Boosting Photoluminescence Rare Earth Glass Analysis

While every precaution has been taken in the preparation of this book, the publisher assumes no responsibility for errors or omissions, or for damages resulting from the use of the information contained herein.

BOOSTING PHOTOLUMINESCENCE RARE EARTH GLASS ANALYSIS

First edition. September 10, 2023.

Copyright © 2023 G. CHANDANA.

ISBN: 979-8223030751

Written by G. CHANDANA.

G. CHANDANA

i | Page

Contents

Chapter – 3 Investigations on Dy^{3+} doped Metal Fluoro Phosphate glasses: Optical studies

Chapter 1 General Introduction

1.1. INTRODUCTION TO GLASSES

Now a days glasses are becoming very important material with different compositions in many preferred forms like lenses, screens, prisms and optical communication fibers which are in demand in regular life. These can be produced by many conventional techniques based on application [1-5].

Glasses with heavy metal elements which are doped with different lanthanide ions have much attention fabrication of optical fiber amplifiers and solid state lasers [4-6]. Also some of these glasses are useful as sensors and second harmonic generators due to their versatile compositional design [7]. So it is very important to study about glass science and is to be a revolutionary area in condensed matter physics [8].

Structural features

Firstly, American Society of Testing Materials (ASTM) has depicted that glass is a definite combination of inorganic materials which under goes fusion. The resultant has been cooled to specific condition for removal of crystallinity. Therefore, glasses are purely non-crystalline and/or amorphous and there is not crystallinity in such materials. The arrangement of atoms in a glassy materials is shown in Fig. 1.1 which have short order regularity.

|Page

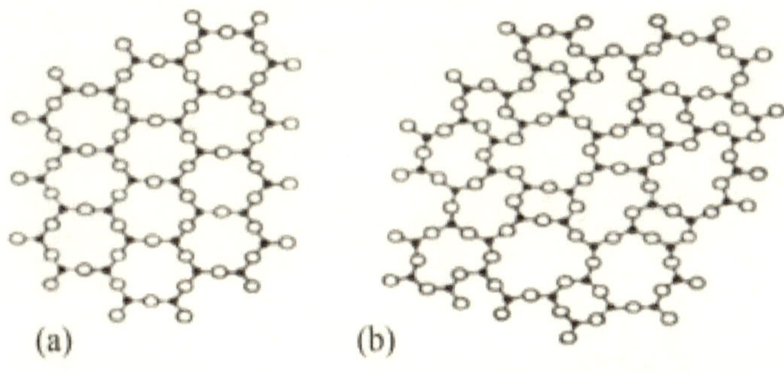

Fig. 1.1: Difference between atomic arrangements in both (a) crystal and (b) glass.

In the network, most of the strong bonding is built with network formers. Silicates, phosphates, Germinates etc are the basic glass network formers. In case of silicate glasses, $(SiO4)^{2-}$ tetrahedrons are the basic molecular units.

To add a rare earth ion (RE^{3+} ion) into that structure, it is needed to add some alkali oxides/fluorides or Zinc oxide or Cadmium oxide which we may called as network modifiers. These network modifiers breaks the glass network and make the feasibility to rare earth ion to enter into the network. The modifier mechanism with and without in the glass network is shown in Fig 1.2.

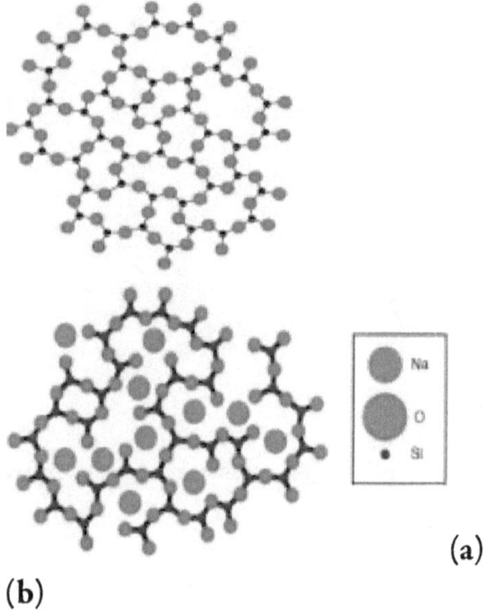

Fig. 1.2: Silicate glass network: (a) without modifier and (b) with modifier.

Thermodynamic features of the glass are shown in Fig.1.3. The transformation of one phase to another phase at particular point is called transition point. In glass also we have a transition point which is called glass transition temperature, represents the transformation from viscous state to solid state [10]. The two parameters which

show considerable changes at glass transition T_g are specific volume and specific heat.

Fig 1.3 shows a phase diagram for glass materials indicating the decrease in volume steadily (state A); and if the cooling rate is slow, represents the initiation of crystallization at melting point Tm, where volume

reduces abruptly (B) and tends to

solid form slowly. Therefore, at rapid cooling, crystallization could be avoided. The rate of cooling temperatures is differing with different kind of materials. Further, $P_2O_5/SiO_2/B_2O_3$ can form glasses with very slow rates of cooling and on quite rapid cooling is required for fluoride glasses.

|Page

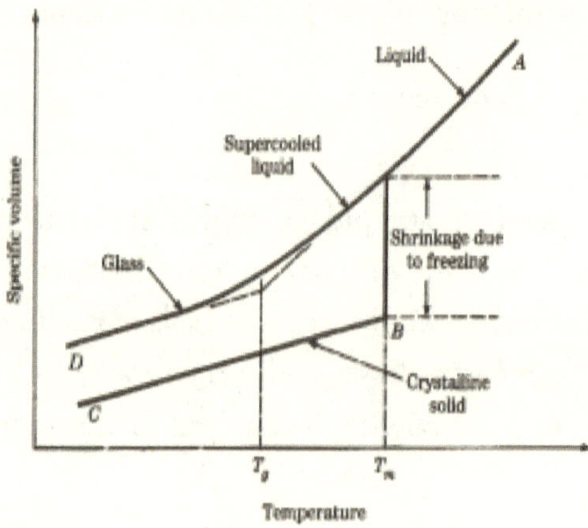

Fig. 1.3. Specific volume vs temperature.

Below the Tg the materials show glassy/amorphous nature. The structure of

rapidly cooled glasses are generally have additional features and prominent than

slowly cooled glass. The isotropic physical properties were present due to absence of

long range network in glass.

In 1945, Douglas [11] reported that if a glass is said to be isotropic, they must

have short range atomic order, thermally, electrically insulating behavior at room

temperatures and had he dependent properties on composition.

1.2. PHOSPHATE GLASS STRUCTURE

Phosphate glasses basically, are the inorganic chains of tetrahedral structured phosphate anion, Fig.1.4 and Fig.1.4 (a) illustrates the formation of sp^3 hybrid orbitals by

the interacting phosphorus outer electrons (3s23p3).

The fifth electron is prop up to the 3d

orbital [12-13] to balance the formation in presence of metal ions.

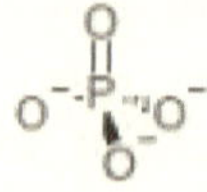

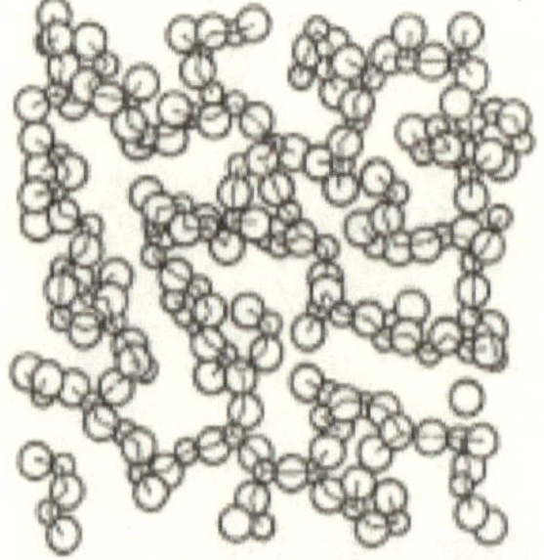

Fig 1.4: The tetrahedral phosphate anion

Fig. 1.4 (a): Illustration of pentavalent phosphorous pentoxide unit –
P and O atoms are represented by small and large circles.

If there are no cations then the shown phosphate tetrahedral
bonds with bridging oxygens to form different phosphate
anions as shown in Fig 1.5.

Fig 1.5: Bonding of phosphate tetrahedral via bridging oxygens as
combinations of linear chains or branches. - Polymerisation of the
phosphate anion.

Basically, tetrahedra are classified with the Q^i terminology.
Originated from silicon glasses [14] however applied to

phosphates [15], where 'i' is number of bridging oxygens per unit tetrahedron. These units are shown in Fig 1.6.

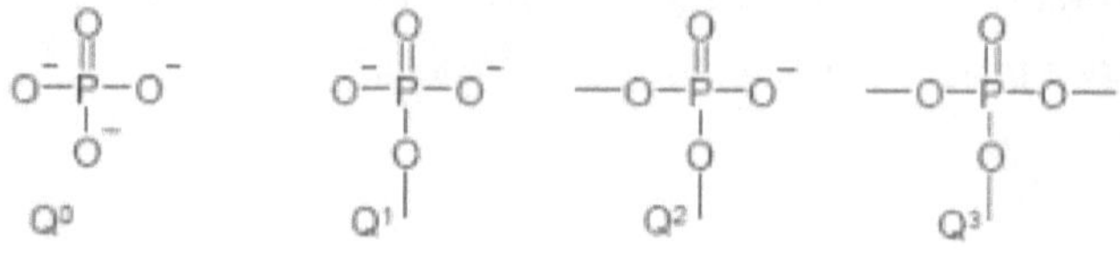

Fig 1.6: The four type of Q^i species of phosphate units.

The Q species is dependent on the concentration of cations included in the total glass composition. If there is a bonding with cations to oxygen then it is not possible to get a bridging oxygen [16]. Pure Phosphorus pentoxide is with Q^3 species and have

highly cross-linked phosphate network. The present

Q2 as non-branched phosphate chains

are due to addition of metal cations [15]. These are called as Meta-Phosphates with one positive charge for every phosphate anion. The addition of much more metal oxides will give rise in removing Q^1 species as decrease in chain length [17]. The total mechanism is expressed in Fig. 1.7 with the concentrations of all the Q species and various names such as polyphosphates, orthophosphates and meta phosphates depending on the concentration of Q species existence.

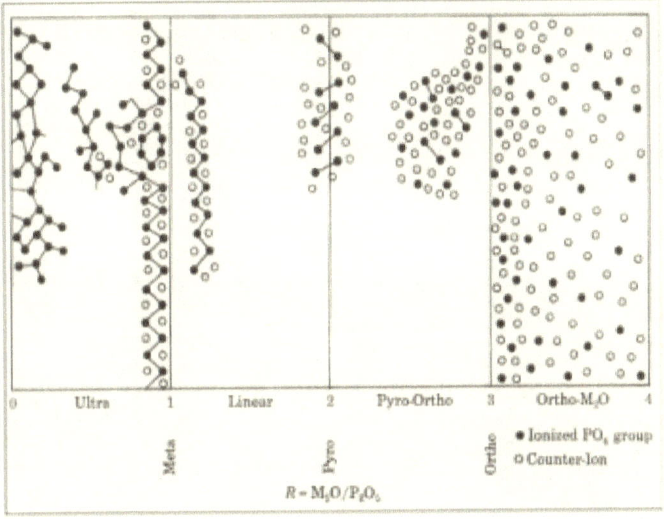

Fig 1.7: Schematic phosphate structures as a function of composition. here linear phosphates are indicated as polyphosphates [15].

So, we can get the phosphate polymerization with the addition of more metal cations which makes the decrease in bridging oxygens to the phosphate anion. Here in some cases water is also considered as phosphate depolymeriser because of formation of Hydroxyl groups [18].

1.3. APPLICATIONS OF PHOSPHATE GLASS

Prominent research work on phosphate glasses improves the vicinity of different applications depending on controlling and understanding. Sometimes, these glasses are useful for vitrifying nuclear waste, medical and sensor applications [19 -23]. Particularly, these phosphate glasses with fluoride content; in case of studies on rare earth ions, shown great efficiency in utilizing as optical and laser materials because

G. CHANDANA

of low absorption [24- 28] and further as glass-metal seals [29]. Further, to treat the trace element deficiencies in cattle and sheep, some compositions of phosphate glasses was used because of their low durability [30-32]. Some many reports are available on the semiconducting properties of phosphate glasses doped with transition metal ions [33-34]. Incorporation of alkali metal ions into phosphate network will benefits the material as conducting materials [35-37], solid electrolytes [37-38] and as membranes for chemical sources of current [39].

1.4. GLASS PREPARATION METHODS

Several glass preparation techniques were proposed Zarzycki [40] to prepare different types of glasses are: (i) thermal evaporation method (ii) melting quenching technique, (iii) chemical reaction method, (iv) electrolytic deposition, (v) gel – desiccation, (vi) reaction amorphization (vii) glow-discharge decomposition, (viii) sputtering, (ix) shockwave transformation, (x) chemical vapour deposition and (xi) shear amorphization. Among these methods, melt quenching technique is easy and comfortable method to produce the amorphous/glass materials.

1.5. RARE EARTH SPECTROSCOPY

By doping lanthanide ions to host may replaces or takes positions at interstitial positions and act as active centers for luminescence upon proper excitation. For periodic atomic arrangement, the crystal field theory and ligand field theory has been developed based on the electronic configuration, symmetry like parameters. The rare earth ions either as RE^{2+} or RE^{3+} have the configurations $4f^n\,5s^2\,5p^6$ or

$4f^{n-1}\,5d\,5s^2\,5p^6$. Table 1.1 shows the electronic configuration and its ground state with observed valance.

Table 1.2: Electronic configurations of lanthanides.

Lanthanide/ Rare Earth element	Atomic number	Electronic configuration [Xe]	Existed valence state	Ground state
La^{3+} - Lanthanum	57	$4f^0$	3	1S0
Ce^{3+} - Cerium	58	$4f^1$	3, 4	2F5/2
Pr^{3+} - Praseodymium	59	$4f^2$	3	3H4
Nd^{3+} - Neodymium	60	$4f^3$	3	4I9/2
Pm^{3+} - Promethium	61	$4f^4$	3	5I4
Sm^{3+} - Samarium	62	$4f^5$	2, 3	6H5/2
$Eu^{2+,3+}$ - Europium	63	$4f^6$	2, 3	7F0
Gd^{3+} - Gadolinium	64	$4f^7$	3	8S7/2
$Tb^{3+,4+}$ - Terbium	65	$4f^8$	3, 4	7F6
Dy^{3+} - Dysprosium	66	$4f^9$	3	6H15/2
Ho^{3+} - Holmium	67	$4f\,10$	3	5I8
Er^{3+} - Erbium	68	$4f\,11$	3	4I15/2
Tm^{3+} - Thulium	69	$4f\,12$	3	3H6
$Yb^{2+,3+}$ - Ytterbium	70	$4f\,13$	2, 3	2F7/2
Lu^{3+} - Lutetium	71	$4f\,14$	3	1S0

The Hund's rule states that the S has low energy for high quantum state, additionally, for the same S to various terms, highest L-angular momentum quantum

number has the low energy; so it explains the filling of $4f$ shells. As a result of spin-

orbit coupling, the spectral terms $_{2S+1}L$ are divided into $^{(2S+1)}L_J$ levels as $J = L + S, L+ (S- 1),, |L - S|$. The predicted ground states of different ions are also given in Table 1.1.

Most of the lanthanide ions have the same chemical properties because 4f electrons will not actively participate in chemical bondings due to the surrounding 5s and 5p electrons [11]. In all the lanthanide ions, the $4f_n$ configuration, the most stable

configurations are $4f0$, $4f7$ and $4f14$; because of empty half filled and filled shells

respectively. Sometimes these will be occurs in divalent and tetravalent states. Eu^{2+} and Tb^{4+} ($4f7$), Ce^{4+} ($4f0$) and Sm^{2+} ($4f6$), Yb^{2+} ($4f14$) are examples. Different valence states for the lanthanide ions are also represented in Table 1.1.

Generally, the lanthanide ions belongs to 4f shell and their ground state is $4fn$

and first excited state is $4f^{n-1}5d$. Basically, $4f$ orbitals are surrounded by the filled

$5s^2 5p^6$ orbitals (Fig. 1.8), and are weakly perturbed by the charge of the surrounding oxygen ligands; so the reason for the existence of unique optical properties of rare earth ions is may be the shielding of $4f$ orbitals [41].

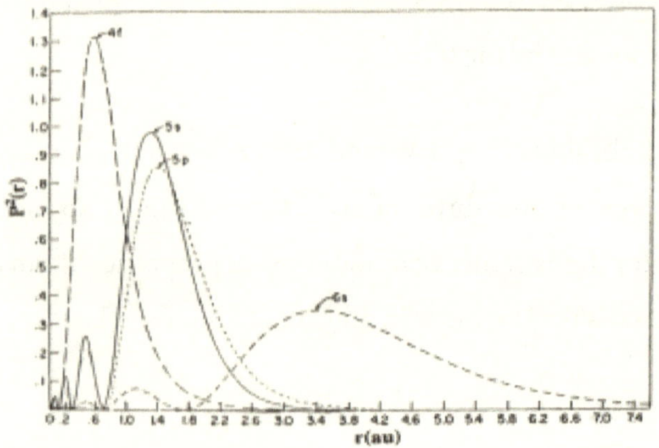

Fig. 1.8: Shielding of unpaired 4f electrons by outer filled 5s^2 and 5p^6 shell electrons.

Based on Dieke [42] presentation, Johns Hopkins group developed the complete

possible set of energy levels and their assignments to various rare earth ions doped in

anhydrous trichlorides, and are shown in Fig. 1.9. Therefore it is very convenient to

determine the J which represents the variations in host.

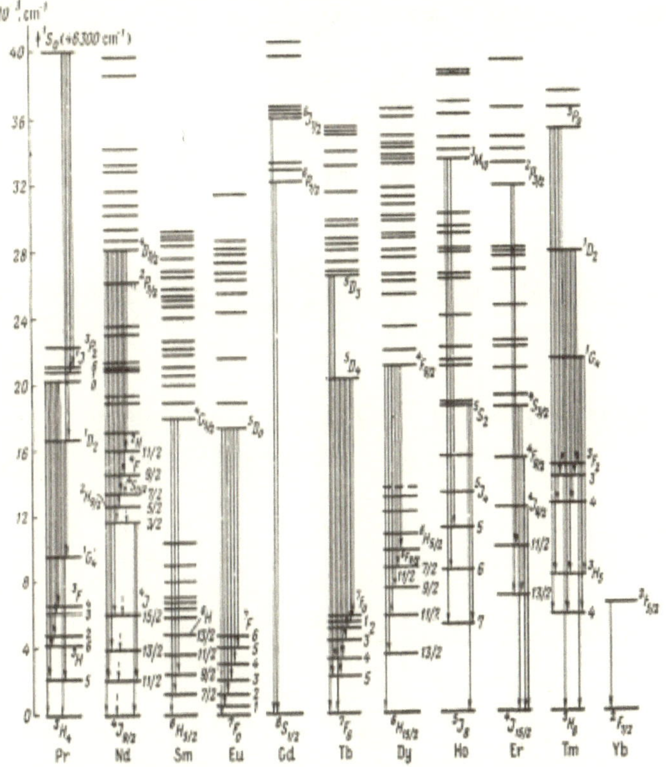

Fig.1.9: Possible energy levels of trivalent lanthanide ions.

The characteristic of rare earth ions interms of colours are explained by Main- Smith [43] by using the transitions of the 4f electrons and the ions with their exhibited colours are given in Table 1.3.

Table 1.3: Colours of the RE^{3+} ions.

$4f^{14-n}$	Colour	$4f^n$
Lu ($4f^{14}$)	Colourless	La ($4f^0$)
Yb ($4f^{13}$)	Colourless	Ce ($4f^1$)
Tm ($4f^{12}$)	Green	Pr ($4f^2$)
Er ($4f^{11}$)	Pink	Nd ($4f^3$)
Ho ($4f^{10}$)	Orange	Pm ($4f^4$)
Dy ($4f^9$)	Yellow	Sm ($4f^5$)
Tb ($4f^8$)	Pale pink	Eu ($4f^6$)
	Colourless	Gd ($4f^7$)

Here trivalent lanthanide ions plays key role in usage of luminescent centers because:

a) Emission of high intense monochromatic light.

b) Sufficient emission lifetimes.

c) They possess many fluorescing states.

d) Their intraconfigurational *f-f* transitions have small uniform line widths.

e) The effect of local fields are considered as perturbations on the free ion energy levels in glassy materials.

f) For energy level analysis, number of theoretical models is validating the excited state dynamics with transition intensities.

1.6. SPECTROSCOPIC PROPERTIES OF RARE EARTHS

Generally, lanthanides are useful for solid state lasers because of its high absorption, emission characteristics. For individual rare earth elements, certain properties like absorption, emission and transitional characteristics are as:

Cerium: Ce^{3+} ($4f1$) has the ground level $^2F_{5/2}$ and the excited level $^2F_{7/2}$. The energy interval for these two states is about ~2000 cm^{-1}, near-ultraviolet intense, Stokes-shifted 5d → 4f emission of Ce^{3+} is possible due to multiphonon emission with pumping.

Praseodymium: Pr^{3+} ($4f2$) is basically used for 1.3 μm telecommunication window.

Apart from this application, this will emit blue, green and red emission lines which will be useful for lasers [44-45].

Neodymium: Nd^{3+} ($4f3$) is one the most important ion among lanthanides. Nd: $Y_3Al_5O_{12}$ (YAG) is commercially available and widely used solid-state laser applications.

From the absorption spectra, most of the peaks be in between 350 nm to 900 nm and exhibits efficient emission of 1.06 μm laser transition [46].

Promethium: The energy levels of Pm^{3+} ($4f4$) ions are very attractive in laser action NIR regions. The radiation is more effective for the basic properties of solid state lasers.

Samarium: Sm^{3+} ($4f5$) ions are very important in glassy hosts for various communication applications, storage and displays. $^{4}G_{5/2}$ is the metastable state for this ion. The laser transitions are takes place from this level. In most of the hosts this ion emits red emission lines [47].

Europium: Eu^{3+} ($4f6$) ion has widely been used in glasses, crystals, phosphors etc., based on different applications because of strong dependence of these ions on environment. The two levels that are $^{7}F0$ level and $^{5}D0$ level are non-degenerate [48]. The Eu^{3+} ions are most prominent in red emitting materials for the applications of fluorescent lamps and colour televisions.

Terbium: Glasses/phosphors doped with Tb^{3+} ($4f8$) ions are useful for optical devices to emit blue and green lights, further used as phosphors in x-ray intensifying screens, projection television tubes and fluorescent lamps. They are also useful for afterglow components by excitation in the intrinsic absorption region of the glassy host [49]. The

$5D4 \rightarrow {}^{7}F5$ transition has higher branching ratio for the

level $^{5}D4$ and the transition will be

as four-level laser at room temperature.

Dysprosium: Dy^{3+} ($4f9$) ions are very important in understanding the bonding nature and the dependence of environment with concentration variations in suitable hosts. This have more excited levels and three emission levels in visible regions upon emission and

excitation wavelengths respectively. The transitions $^4F_{9/2} \rightarrow {}^6H_{13/2}$, $^4F_{9/2} \rightarrow {}^6H_{15/2}$ and $^4F_{9/2}$

$\rightarrow {}^6H_{11/2}$ are in blue, yellow and red regions respectively at 485 nm, 575 nm and 663 nm. Here $^4F_{9/2} \rightarrow {}^6H_{13/2}$ is hypersensitive transition (1'L $=$ 2 and 1'J $=$ 2). The intensity is strongly depends on the host [50] and have many optical applications.

The characteristic colours of the rare earth ions in the visible region due to their emission transition as presented in Table 1.4.

Table 1.4: Important colours emitted by certain of RE^{3+} ions.

RE ion	Emission Wavelength (nm)	Emission transition	Emission colour
Pr3+	610-630	$1D_2 \rightarrow 3H_4$	Red
Sm3+	600-610	$4G_{5/2} \rightarrow 6H_{7/2}$	Orange red
Eu3+	610–630	$5D_0 \rightarrow 7F_2$	Red
Tb3+	535-550	$5D_4 \rightarrow 7F_5$	Green
Dy3+	470-500	$4F_{9/2} \rightarrow H_{15/2}$	
	570 -600	$6F_{15/2} \rightarrow 6F_{11/2}$	White
Ho3+	525-540	$5S_2 \rightarrow 5I_8$	Green
Er3+	535-550	$4S_{3/2} \rightarrow 4I_{15/2}$	Green
Tm3+	460-480	$1G_4 \rightarrow 3H_6$	Blue

1.7. ANALYSIS OF OPTICAL SPECTRA

It is important to understand the electronic energy level structure to analyze the luminescence behavior or rare earth ions. This structural changes can be determined by the interaction of 4f electrons with its surroundings.

1.7.1. Energy level analysis

Energy level structure is a result of several interactions with outer electrons. May be the interactions are either electron-electron interaction or electron-surroundings interaction for the lanthanides. Therefore, it is convenient to use the effective operator model [64] to estimate the interaction between f-f and f-surroundings. The parameter Hamiltonian ($\hat{H}$) which elucidates the energy level structure of lanthanides in any host environment can be expressed as given in Eq. (1.1). The free-ion Hamiltonian ($\hat{H}_{FI}$) is a composition of – two body electrostatic Tree's parameters, Judd parameters and spin-other orbit interaction parameters indicating interactions can be written as follows [66- 67].

The zero-order term, H_0 in the free-ion Hamiltonian (HFI) represents the shift in entire configuration as given by $EAVG$ [65]. The columbic interaction H_{e-e} between the $4f$ electrons is described with the Slater integral, F^k (k = 2,4,6). The spin-orbit interaction H_{s-}

o is represented by several terms namely the spin-orbit

coupling (the coupling constant, ξ)

splits the terms into $^{2S+1}L_J$ states. The effective free-ion Hamiltonian ($H^\wedge$), comprising of two body electrostatic Trees parameters, Judd parameters and spin-other orbit interaction parameters indicating interactions can be written as follows [66-67]

$I.$ k so

$$H^\wedge FI = EAVG +$$

$$Fk f^\wedge + 4f A^\wedge$$

$$k$$

$$+ L^{\wedge}(L^{\wedge} + 1) + G^{\wedge}(G_2) + G^{\wedge}(R_7) +$$

$$\mathbf{I}.T_i t^{\wedge} + \mathbf{I}.P_k p^{\wedge} + \mathbf{I}.M_j m^{\wedge}$$

$$(1.3)$$

$$i\,k\,j$$

Where the operators $(f^{\wedge}, A^{\wedge}, L^{\wedge}, G^{\wedge}, t^{\wedge}, p^{\wedge}, m^{\wedge}$

) correspond to the angular integrals and

$$k\,so\,i\,k\,j$$

allied parameters. By using the standard least square fit, the correlation between experimental and calculated energy levels were obtained and the free-ion parameters,

rms deviation (σrms) are used as a quality parameter of the fit. The σrms is defined as [68- 69]

$$\sigma_{rms} = \sqrt{\frac{\sum_{i=1}^{P}\left(E_i^{exp} - E_i^{cal}\right)^2}{P}}$$

$$(1.4)$$

Where E_{cal} and E_{exp} are the calculated and experimental

energies for level i and P

i

indicate the total number of experimental levels used in energy level fit.

1.7.2. Spectral Intensities and Judd-Ofelt theory

Judd and Ofelt [57-58] described a theoretical formulation for the intensities of absorption bands of rare earth ions in solid hosts in 1962. The Judd-Ofelt theory is derived from a static, free-ion and a single configuration approximation where the activator ion dependent on host matrix through a static electric field. In a host, for an ion, the combination of energy states from the opposite parity configurations results the existence of electric dipole transitions and the transition probability depends on these combination of states. The Judd-Ofelt (J-O) theory radiative parameters of the emission levels with both absorption spectrum and the fluorescence spectrum.

Absorption oscillator strengths

Depending on J-O theory, the oscillator strength for a transition can be given as:

$$f(\backslash jJ$$

$$\backslash jJ\ \text{I I} = 8n\ _2mcv\ 1(n_2 + 2)_2$$

$$\backslash jJ$$

$$\backslash jJ\ \text{I I} +$$

$$\backslash jJ$$

$$\backslash jJ\ \text{I I l}$$

(1.5)

cal

$J, J)$
$3h\,(2J+1)\,\mathrm{I}\,9n$

$S_{ed}(J;$

$J)\,n\,S_{md}(J;$

$J)1$

J

└───── Where m is the electron mass, h is the Plank's constant, c is the speed of light, the

degeneracy of the ground state is $(2J+1)$,

$$(n_2+2)_2$$

$$\text{───}9n$$

is Lorentz local field correction

factor. Here the rare earth ions in a dielectric medium of refractive index n . Further, S_{ed}

-electric dipole and S_{md} -magnetic dipole line strengths respectively and are given by:

S_{ed}

$$(|jJJ; |jJ \, IJ \, I) = e_2$$

$$I._O{}^{\prime\prime}A$$

$${}^{\prime\prime}A = 2,4,6$$

$$2$$

$$\rangle\!\langle\!\rangle\!\langle|_{jJJ} \, U^{\prime\prime A} \, |jJ \, IJ \, I$$

$$(1.6)$$

$$S(|jJ \, |jJ \, I \, I =$$

$$2$$

$$\rangle\!\langle\!\rangle\!\langle\left|\frac{e^2 h^2}{16 n^2 m^2 c^2}\right|\!\!\langle \, |jJ + |jJ \, I \, I$$

$${}_{md}J; J)$$

$$JL \, 2SJ$$

$$(1.7)$$

The three intensity parameters O''_A ($''A$ = 2,4,6) are known as phenomenological Judd-

Ofelt parameters and are sensitive to any structural changes.

$$\langle jJ | U^{''A} | jJ IJ I \rangle$$

are the

reduced matrix elements of the unit tensor operator of rank $''A$ and does dependent on

host. The experimental oscillator strength

f_{exp} of a transition [70] is expressed by

$$f_{exp} = \frac{2.303 mc_2}{Nn\, e_2}$$

$$f_a (v)\, dv = 4.318x10_{-9}$$

$$f_a (v)\, dv$$

(1.8)

Where m- mass of an electron and e- charge of an electron, N- Avagadro's number, c-

velocity of light, and

$a(v)$

is the molar absorptivity of a band as a function of

wavenumber (cm^{-1}). It is related to the area under the absorption peak and is a dimensionless quantity. The molar absorptivity at a given wave number can be calculated

from the Beer-Lambert's law expressed as:

$$\underline{\qquad}a(v) = 1 \log I_0$$

(1.9)

$$Cl\,I$$

Where l -light path in absorbing medium (cm), C-concentration of the rare earth (RE^{3+}) ions (mol/l), and $\log(I_0/I)$ is known as optical density or absorptivity. According to the J- O theory, calculated oscillator strengths (Eq. 1.5) and the experimentally measured one

(Eq. 1.8) should be equal. The intensity parameters

$O^{\,\prime\prime\prime}\!A$ are estimated through a least

squares fitting of the experimental oscillator strengths. The same parameters are then used to calculate the radiative transition probabilities.

Emission spectra

The Judd-Ofelt parameters obtained from the absorption measurements can be used to describe the radiative properties of different excited fluorescent levels. The spontaneous emission probability for an electric dipole transition is expressed as [71-72].

$$\llcorner 64n_{4v_3} 1 n \left(n_2 + 2 \right)_2 1$$

$$=\!=\!=$$

$$A_R \left(|jJJ, |jJ \, IJ \, I \right) =$$

$$3h \left(2J + 1 \right) I 9$$

$$S \left(|jJJ, |jJ \, IJ \, I \right) + n_3 S \left(|jJJ, |jJ \, IJ \, I \right) 1 \quad (1.10)$$

$$_{ed} \qquad\qquad _{md} 1J$$

The total transition probability from an initial $|jJJ$ manifold to a final manifold $|jJJ \, I$ is then

given by

$$A_T \left(|jJJ \right) = \mathbf{I}. A_R \left(|jJJ; |jJ \, IJ \, I \right)$$

$$|jJ \, IJ \, I$$

$$(1.11)$$

For an excited level, the radiative lifetime T_R is

$$T_R(|jJJ) =$$

$$\frac{1}{A_T(|jJJ)}$$

(1.12)

The branching ratio is

$$_R(|jJJ, |jJ \, IJ \, I) = \frac{A(|jJJ, |jJ \, IJ \, I)}{A_T(|jJJ)}$$

(1.13)

Finally, the stimulated emission cross-section a_e for a transition from $|jJJ$ to $|jJ \, IJ \, I$ is

given as

$$''A_4$$

$$a(|jJJ, |jJ \, IJ \, I) = {}_P A(|jJJ, |jJ \, IJ \, I)$$

(1.14)

$$\nu_e \; 8n \; cn_2 \; 1'''A \; _R$$

Where $''A_P$ is the wavelength of the spectral line. $1'''A_P$ represents an effective bandwidth

obtained by the ratio of integrated intensity of the emission band to the intensity at the peak of the band and can be evaluated by fitting with a Gaussian function.

1.8. EXCITED STATE DYNAMICS

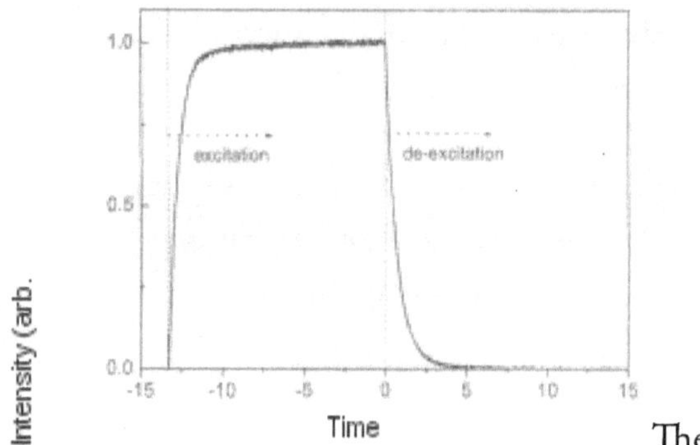

The mechanisms involved in excitation of RE ions can be studied by excitation and de-excitation. Time-resolved intensity spectrum is shown in Fig. 1.8. Which shows the excitation and de-excitation mechanisms.

Fig. 1.8: Time-resolved excitation and de-excitation mechanisms of RE^{3+} ions.

1.8.1. Single-exponential and experimental lifetimes

Fluorescence decay measurements are useful to determine the excited state lifetimes (T). The lifetime is of the order of 10^{-8} s. For forbidden transitions the lifetime is 10^{-3} s. The interaction between rare earth ions are very low at lower

concentrations therefore, the decay curves can be fitted into a single exponential function which represents the energy transfer in between dopant ions as negligible. The

fluorescence intensity as a function of time is expressed as:

$-t / T$

$$I(t) = I0 \, e \, \exp$$

(1.19)

Where $I0$ is the fluorescence intensity, T_{exp} signifies the lifetime of the excited state. The

probability of a spontaneous emission can also be represented as reciprocal of the lifetime.

1.8.2. Non-radiative relaxation

In non-radiative process the rare earth ions mainly relaxes at lower energy states. All the deviations obtained from a single exponential decay. If T_{exp} is the experimentally

measured lifetime, then the total decay rate $(1/T_{exp})$ is

the combination of radiative (AR)

decay rate and non-radiative (WNR) decay rates.

$$T1 = A + W$$

—

(1.20)

R_{m}^{NR}

The non-radiative decay rates W_{NR} related to the quenching of experimental lifetime. The types of these decay rates as

$$W_{NR} = W_{MPR} + W_{ET} + W_{CQ} + W_{OH}$$

(1.21)

Where W_{MPR}, - NR decay rate corresponding to multi-phonon relaxation, W_{ET}, - energy transfer between donor to acceptor or donor to donor; W_{OH} - Hydroxyl groups and W_{CQ} – Concentration Quenching.

Multiphonon de-excitation

In a multiphonon de-excitation, phonon may release by relaxation and it is depending on the electron-phonon coupling strength. To calculate the multiphonon decay rate [75], a single configurational coordinate model. The multiphonon relaxation rate (MPR) can be expressed as

$$W_{MPR} = B\exp\left(- 1'E\right)$$

(1.22)

Where the parameters B and α depend on the composition of the host, but independent of

the RE^{3+} ion and $1'E$ is the energy gap. In fact, most of the energetic phonons are accountable for the non-radiative decay. Logarithm of the multiphonon decay rate

decreases linearly with the energy gap. The average phonon energies (hw) of some of the network formers are given in Table 1.7.

Table 1.7: Average phonon energies ($\hbar\omega$) of the glass matrices.

Glass matrix	hw (cm^{-1})
Phosphate glass	1200
Borate glass	1400
Germanate glass	900
Silicate glass	1100
Tellurite glass	700

Concentration quenching

When the activator (acceptor) concentration increases, the distance between activator ions decreases and the energy may transfer from lattice to sites. This causes the loss in non-radiative energy [76]. These sites/lattices, we can call them as impurities, surface sites, defects etc. Due to that, a decrease in emission intensity occurred. So concentration quenching is a major factor which depends on photoluminescence intensity.

1.9. CIE- COLOR COORDINATES

In solid state displays, it is necessary to control the colours. It is well known that combination of three or more colours will generate the white light. For the present study concern it is a fact that the combination of blue and yellow with or without other colour may produce white light [77-80]. The white light that could be obtained by the emission of Dy^{3+}: CDP glass has been estimated interms of CIE colour coordinates and these were calculated by using the below expressions from the tri-stimulus values.

$$\frac{X}{X+Y+Z} = x \qquad (1.23)$$

$$\frac{Y}{X+Y+Z} = y \qquad (1.24)$$

Where X, Y and Z are the colour matching functions for primary red, green and blue colours. The colour matching functions described by the following equations [81].

$$\_X = \int x(''A)P(''A)d''A$$

$$''A$$

$$\_Y = \int y(''A)P(''A)d''A$$

$$''A$$

$$\_Z = \int z\,(''A)P(''A)d''A$$

$$''A$$

(1.25)

(1.26)

(1.27)

The Commission Internationale de l'Eclairage (CIE) 1931 chromaticity diagram is shown in Fig. 1.9 with all monochromatic colour coordinates.

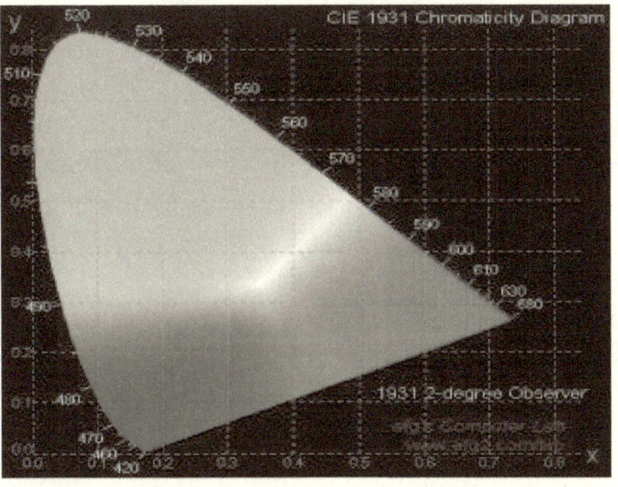

Fig. 1.9: CIE 1931 xy chromaticity diagram

The colour coordinates of a source can be estimated with the color purity and is given by

$$\frac{\sqrt{(x - x_{ii})^2 + (y - y_{i})^2}}{\sqrt{(x_{if} - x_{ii})^2 + (y_{d} - y)^2}_{ee}} \quad \text{Color purity} = (1.28)$$

Where $(x, y), (x_{ee}, y_{ee})$ are the chromaticity coordinates of the emission light.

References

[1] Poirier G, Ottoboni FS, Castro Cassanjes F, Remonte Á, Messaddeq Y, Ribeiro SJ. Redox behavior of molybdenum and tungsten in phosphate glasses. The Journal of Physical Chemistry B. 2008 ;112(15):4481-7.

[2] Ohtsuki M, Tamura R, Takeuchi S, Yoda S, Ohmura T. Hard metallic glass of tungsten-based alloy. Applied physics letters. 2004 ;84(24):4911-3.

[3] Engelhardt MA, Jaswal SS, Sellmyer DJ. Photoemission and electronic structure of tungsten-based metallic glasses and alloys. Physical Review B. 1991;44(23):12671.

[4] Wachtler M, Speghini A, Gatterer K, Fritzer HP, Ajo D, Bettinelli M. Optical properties of rare-earth ions in lead germanate glasses. Journal of the American Ceramic Society. 1998, 81(8):2045-52.

[5] Layne CB, Lowdermilk WH, Weber MJ. Multiphonon relaxation of rare-earth ions in oxide glasses. Physical Review B. 1977, 16(1):10.

[6] Ebendorff-Heidepriem H, Ehrt D, Bettinelli M, Speghini A. Spectroscopic properties of rare-earth ions in heavy metal oxide and phosphate-containing glasses. InRare-Earth-Doped Materials and Devices III 1999 (Vol. 3622, pp. 19- 30). International Society for Optics and Photonics.

[7] Murugan GS, Suzuki T, Ohishi Y. Tellurite glasses for ultrabroadband fiber Raman amplifiers. Applied Physics Letters. 2005, 86(16):161109.

[8] J. Zarzycki, Glasses and Amorphous Materials, in: R.W. Cahn, P. Haasen, E.J. Kramer (Eds.), Material Science and Technology, Vol. 9, Basel, New York, 1991.

[9] Am. Soc. Testing Mater., ASTM C 162-56, ASTM stand. Part 13, 1965.

[10] Debenedetti PG, Stillinger FH. Supercooled liquids and the glass transition. Nature. 2001 410 (6825) 259-67.

[11] R.W. Douglas, J. Sci. Instrum. 22 (1945) 81.

[12] Cruickshank DW. 1077. The rôle of 3 d-orbitals in π-bonds between (a) silicon, phosphorus, sulphur, or chlorine and (b) oxygen or nitrogen. Journal of the Chemical Society (Resumed). 1961:5486-504.

[13] Mitchell KA. Use of outer d orbitals in bonding. Chemical Reviews. 1969 69(2) 157-78.

[14] Lippmaa E, Maegi M+, Samoson A, Engelhardt G, Grimmer AR. Structural studies of silicates by solid-state high-resolution silicon-29 NMR. Journal of the American Chemical Society. 1980, 102(15): 4889-93.

[15] J. R. Van Wazer, "Phosphorus and its Compounds", London, Interscience Publishers Ltd., (1958).

[16] S. W. Martin, European J. Solid State Inorg. Chem., 28 (1991) 163-205.

[17] Wazer JR. Structure and properties of the condensed phosphates. III. Solubility fractionation and other solubility studies. Journal of the American Chemical Society. 1950, 72(2), 647-55.

[18] Brow RK, Kirkpatrick RJ, Turner GL. The short range structure of sodium phosphate glasses I. MAS NMR studies. Journal of Non-crystalline solids. 1990 116(1) 39-45.

[19] Mesko MG, Day DE, Bunker BC. Immobilization of CsCl and SrF2 in iron phosphate glass. Waste Management. 2000 20(4) 271-8.

[20] Huang W, Day DE, Ray CS, Kim CW, Mogus-Milankovic A. Vitrification of high chrome oxide nuclear waste in iron phosphate glasses. Journal of nuclear materials. 2004 Apr 1; 327(1):46-57.

[21] W. H.Huang, D. E. Day, C. S. Ray, C. W. Kim and S. T. D. Reis, Glass Sci. and Tech.. 77 (2004) 203-210.

[22] C. W. Kim and D. E. Day, Am. Chem. Soc., 227 (2004) U1044-U1045.

[23] W. H. Huang, N. Zhou, D. E. Day and C. S. Ray, J. Inorg. Mat., 20 (2005) 842- 850.

[24] Ebendorff-Heidepriem H, Ehrt D. Formation and UV absorption of cerium, europium and terbium ions in different valencies in glasses. Optical Materials. 2000 15(1) 7-25.

[25] Philipps JF, Töpfer T, Ebendorff-Heidepriem H, Ehrt D, Sauerbrey R. Spectroscopic and lasing properties of Er^{3+}: Yb^{3+}-doped fluoride phosphate glasses. Applied Physics B. 2001 72(4) 399-405.

[26] Ebendorff-Heidepriem H, Ehrt D. Effect of europium ions on X-ray-induced defect formation in phosphate containing glasses. Optical Materials. 2002 19(3) 351-63.

[27] H. Ebendorff-Heidepriem, C. Riziotis and E. R. Taylor, Glass Sci. Tech., 75 (2002) 54-59.

[28] Philipps JF, Töpfer T, Ebendorff-Heidepriem H, Ehrt D, Sauerbrey R. Energy transfer and upconversion in erbium–ytterbium-doped fluoride phosphate glasses. Applied Physics B. 2002, 74(3), 233-6.

[29] Wei TY, Hu Y, Hwa LG. Structure and elastic properties of low-temperature sealing phosphate glasses. Journal of non-crystalline solids. 2001, 288(1-3), 140-7.

[30] W. M. Allen, B. F. Sansom, C. F. Drake and D. C. Davies, Veter. Sci. Comm., 2 (1978) 73-75.

[31] Allen WM, Sansom BF, Gleed PT, Mallinson CB, Drake CF. Boluses of controlled release glass for supplementing ruminants with copper. The Veterinary Record. 1984,115(3):55-7.

[32] Allen WM, Sansom BF, Mallinson CB, Stebbings RJ, Drake CF. Boluses of controlled release glass for supplementing ruminants with cobalt. The Veterinary record. 1985, 116(7):175-7.

[33] Owen AE. Semiconducting glasses part 1: glass as an electronic conductor. Contemporary Physics. 1970, 11(3), 227-55.

[34] Murawski L, Chung CH, Mackenzie JD. Electrical properties of semiconducting oxide glasses. Journal of non-crystalline solids. 1979, 32(1-3), 91-104.

[35] Otto K. Electrical conductivity of SiO_2-B_2O_3 glasses containing lithium or sodium. Phys. Chem. Glasses. 1966, 7(1), 29-37.

[36] S.W.Martin, J.Am.Ceram.Soc., 74 (1991) 1967.

[37] S.Poisson, P.Berthet, A.Belkehir and A.Rulmont,Proc.XAFS8[th]Conf.,Berlin. 1994.

[38] Rao DS, Karat PP, Parvathi B. Dc conductivity of the P_2O_5-Na_2O-ZnO glass system. Journal of Materials Science Letters. 1990 Jul;9(7):748-9.

[39] I.M. Bushueva, L.F. Pendenko, L.P.Kalmykova and S.Eghov, Vestn.Leuingr. Univ.Fiz.Chi., 4 (1978)116.

[40] Zarzycki J. Glasses and the vitreous state. Cambridge university press; 1991.

[41] Freeman AJ, Watson RE. Theoretical investigation of some magnetic and spectroscopic properties of rare-earth ions. Physical Review. 1962 Sep 15;127(6):2058.

[42] Dieke GH. Spectroscopic observations on maser materials. Advances in Quantum Electronics. 1961:164.

[43] Smith JM. The Rare Earths. Nature. 1927, 120(3025):583-4.

[44] Liu X, Kale BB, Tikhomirov VK, Jha A. Reduction of OH$^-$-related photoluminescence quenching in Pr^{3+}-doped GeS2-based glasses by means of purification. Journal of non-crystalline solids. 1999 Oct 2;256:294-8.

[45] R. Balda, J. Fernandez, A. de Pablos and J.M. Fdez – Navarro, J. Phys: Condens. Matter 11 (1999) 12.

[46]   D.C.Brown:High-Peak-PowerNd:GlassLaserSystems (Springer,Berlin,1981),Ch.3.

[47] Suhasini T, Kumar JS, Sasikala T, Jang K, Lee HS, Jayasimhadri M, Jeong JH, Yi SS, Moorthy LR. Absorption and fluorescence properties of Sm^{3+} ions in fluoride containing phosphate glasses. Optical Materials. 2009, 31(8), 1167-72.

[48] V. Lavin, U.R. Rodriguez – Mendoza, I.R. Martin and V.D. Rodriguez, J. Non – Cryst. Solids 319 (2003) 206.

[49] B.C. Jamalaiah, J. Suresh Kumar, A. Mohan Babu, T. Sasikala, L. Rama Moorthy,

Physica B 404 (2009) 2020

[50] A. Mohan Babu, B.C. Jamalaiah, J. Suresh Kumar, T. Sasikala, L. Rama Moorthy,

Journal of Alloys and Compounds 509 (2011) 457

[51] M. Shojiya and Y. Kawamoto, J. Appl. Phys., 89 (9) (2004) 4944.

[52] Y.S. Han, J. Heo and Y.B. Shin, J. Non – Cryst. Solids, 316 (2003) 302.

[53] K.-S. Lim, P. Babu, C.K. Jayasankar, S.K. Lee, V.T. Pham, H.J. Seo, J. Alloys. Compd. 385 (2004) 12.

[54] B. Henderson, R.H. Bartram, Crystal field engineering of solid state laser materials, Cambridge University Press, 2000.

[55] B. Henderson, G.F. Imbusch, Optical spectroscopy of inorganic solids, Oxford University Press, 1989.

[56] B. Henderson, Contem. Phys. 43 (2002) 273. [57] B.R. Judd, Phys. Rev. 127 (1962) 750.

[58] G.S. Ofelt, J. Chem. Phys. 37 (1962) 511.

[59] S. Tanabe, T. Ohyagi, N.Soga, T. Hanada, Phys. Rev. B 46 (1992) 3305.

[60] S.N. Misra, J. Sci. Ind. Res. 44 (1985) 366.

[61] C.K. Jørgensen, B.R. Judd, Mol. Phys. 8 (1964) 281.

[62] D.G. Karraker, Inorg. Chem. 6 (1967) 1863.

[63] G.R. Choppin, D.E. Henrie, K. Buijs, Inorg. Chem. 5 (1966) 1743.

[64] B.G. Wybourne, "Spectroscopic Properties of Rare Earths", John Wiley, New York, 1965.

[65] G. W. Burdick, C. K. Jayasankar, F. S. Richardson, M. F. Reid, Phys. Rev. B 50 (1994) 16309.

[66] H.A. Kramers, Proc. Acad. Amsterdam 33 (1930) 959

[67] W.T.Carnall, G.L.Goodman, K.Rajnak, R.S. Rana, J. Chem. Phys. 90 (1989) 3443.

[68] S.A. Saleem, B.C. Jamalaiah, A. Mohan Babu, K. Pavani, L. Rama Moorthy, Journal of Rare Earths 28 (2010) 189.

[69] C.A.Morrison, R.P.Leavitt, "Handbook on the Physics and Chemistry of Rare Earths", Ed. K. A. Gschneidner Jr., L. Eyring, North-Holland, Amsterdam, Vol. 5, 1982, p. 461.

[70] C. Görler-Walrand, K. Binnemans, Handbook on the Physics and Chemistry of Rare Earths, Ed. K. A.

Gschneidner Jr. and L. Eyring, North-Holland, Amsterdam, 1998, Vol. 25, p.101.

[71] C.W. Nielson, G.F. Koster, Spectroscopic coefficients for p^n, d^n, and f^n configurations, MIT Press, Cambridge, Mass., 1964.

[72] M. Rotenberg, R. Bivins, N. Metropolis, J.R. Wooten, The 3j and 6j symbols, MIT Press, Cambridge, Mass., 1959.

[73] D.E. McCumber, Phys. Rev. A 134 (1964) 299.

[74] M.J. Miniscalco, R.S. Quimby, Opt. Lett.16 (1991) 258.

[75] W.M. Yen, S. Shionoya, H. Yamamoto, Phosphor handbook, CRC Press, Taylor & Francis Group, 2006.

G. CHANDANA

[76] D.L. Dexter, J. Schulaman, J. Chem. Phys. 22 (1954) 1063. [77] B. Liu,C. Shi, Z. Qi, Appl. Phys. Lett. 63 (1993) 3268-3270.

[78] J. Kuang, Y. Liu, J. Zhang, J. Solid State Chem. 179 (2006) 266-269.

[79] L.A. Diaz-Torres, E.De La Rosa, P. Salas, V.H. Romero, C. Angeles-Chavez, J. Solid State Chem. 181 (2008) 75-80.

[80] V. Lavin, F. Lahoz, I.R. Martin, U.R. Rodriguez-Mendoza, in: R.Balda (Eds.), Photonic Glasses, Research Signpost, Trivandrum, India, 2006, pp. 115-149.

[81] E. Fred Schubert, Light-Emitting Diodes (2nd edition, Cambridge University Press, 2006.

******

Chapter 2 Experimental Methods

2.1. INTRODUCTION

In this present chapter, the details of experimental methods used to prepare glass, physical measurements, Optical absorption, photoluminescence, Fourier Transform Infrared Spectra of different rare earth doped in cadmium zinc phosphate glasses were discussed. Selection of glass composition has been made for the optical applications. As the optical performance is depends on glass structure, composition, optical quality, durability and efficiency, these glasses have been chosen for the present study.

2.2. GLASS PREPARATION

The most convenient way to prepare the glasses is the melt quenching technique. So, this method was used to prepare the present glasses. After several attempts, the aimed Cd-Pb-Na Fluoro phosphate glasses were prepared with different compositions as shown below:

SERIES 1:

59.9 P_2O_5 – 10CdF_2 – 15PbF_2 – 15NaF_2 – 0.1 Dy_2O_3

59.7 P_2O_5 – 10CdF_2 – 15PbF_2 – 15NaF_2 – 0.3 Dy_2O_3

59.5 P_2O_5 – 10CdF_2 – 15PbF_2 – 15NaF_2 – 0.5 Dy_2O_3

58.5 P_2O_5 – 10CdF2 – 15PbF2 – 15NaF2 – 0.5 Dy_2O_3
+1MgO

SERIES 2:

59.9 P2O5 – 10CdF2 – 15PbF2 – 15NaF2 – 0.1 Sm2O3

59.7 P2O5 – 10CdF2 – 15PbF2 – 15NaF2 – 0.3 Sm2O3

59.5 P2O5 – 10CdF2 – 15PbF2 – 15NaF2 – 0.5 Sm2O3

58.5 P2O5 – 10CdF2 – 15PbF2 – 15NaF2 – 0.5 Sm2O3 +1MgO

SERIES 3:

59.9 P2O5 – 10CdF2 – 15PbF2 – 15NaF2 – 0.1 Pr6O11

59.7 P2O5 – 10CdF2 – 15PbF2 – 15NaF2 – 0.3 Pr6O11

59.5 P2O5 – 10CdF2 – 15PbF2 – 15NaF2 – 0.5 Pr6O11

58.5 P2O5 – 10CdF2 – 15PbF2 – 15NaF2 – 0.5 Pr6O11 +1MgO

SERIES 4: UV and Laser irradiated

59.5 P2O5 – 10CdF2 – 15PbF2 – 15NaF2 – 0.5Dy2O3

59.5 P2O5 – 10CdF2 – 15PbF2 – 15NaF2 – 0.5Pr6O11

59.5 P2O5 – 10CdF2 – 15PbF2 – 15NaF2– 0.5Sm2O3

Glasses were prepared from research grade **Sm2O3**, **Pr6O11**, **Dy2O3**, CdF2, PbF2, NaF and P2O5 by mixing them thoroughly in an porcelain mortar and melting in porcelain crucible for 1.5 hours at 1150 ^{0}C at an ambient atmosphere for a proper composition given below. The molten mixture is then quenched to room temperature suddenly and poured on preheated brass plates and annealed at 250 ^{0}C for 5 hours to avoid the breaking due to thermal strains.

2.3. PHYSICAL PROPERTIES

Estimation of Physical properties such as density, thickness, refractive index and concentration of the rare earth ions are important to characterize the present rare earth ion doped Cd-Zn phosphate glasses.

Thickness: By using screw gauge, thicknesses (l) for all the samples were measured.

Refractive index: For refractive index measurements were done by using Medimeas - Abbe refractometer with one bromophenophtalene as contact liquid for the measurement.

Density: By Using Archimede's method, the densities (d) of the prepared glasses were estimated. Density is estimated by using the following formula. Here the immersion liquid is distilled water. The measurement was done at room temperature.

———

$$d = (\, a \, 1 \text{ gm/cc} \quad (2.1)$$

I $a - b$ l

)

Where 'a'- sample weight in air, 'b' is the sample weight in distilled water

Concentration: The rare earth (RE^{3+}) ion concentration (C) in the glass (in mol/litre) was found using the expression,

$$\_\_C = y\, MW$$

x d x 1000

$$\_x$$

(2.2)

Where y= mass of the rare earth salt

x = total mass of the composition

d = is the density of the glass sample and

MW = molecular weight of the rare earth salt.

The rare-earth element concentration in mol/l can be transformed into ions/cm^3 by multiplying it with Avagadro's number N.

2.4. X-RAY DIFFRACTOMETRY

X-ray Diffraction (XRD) is well known method which uses a monochromatic X- rays is directed onto powder material placed in a sample holder. The sample-diffracted X- rays are measured. The data received from instrument enables the information associated with atomic structure of the material [1].

X-ray diffraction studies have been used to estimate/identify the degree of crystalline and amorphous nature of glasses/ materials. XRD patterns of the glass samples was recorded by Shimadzu X-ray diffractometer. The instrument have CuK radiation source operatable at 40kV and 30mA. The resultant X-ray diffraction is a function of angle 2θ [2].

Fig 2 .1: Shimadzu X-Ray diffractometer

Bragg's diffraction law $n\lambda=2d\sin\theta$ is the base for X-ray diffraction and it is familiar to calculate the interplanar distance and the corresponding angles. In this present work, XRD patterns obtained have no such significant peaks but had a broad diffusion which corresponds to the existence of amorphous/glass nature of the as prepared cadmium zinc phosphate glass systems. One of the XRD pattern is shown below as all are similar [2].

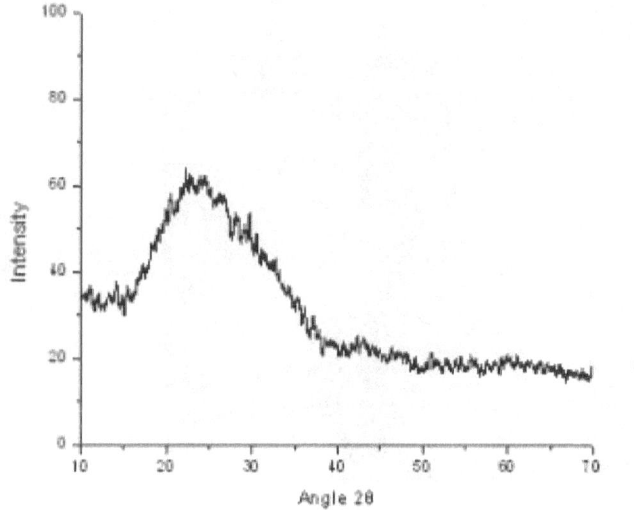

Fig 2.1a: XRD pattern of Cadmium Zinc phosphate glass (CdP)

2.5. OPTICAL ABSORPTION SPECTRA

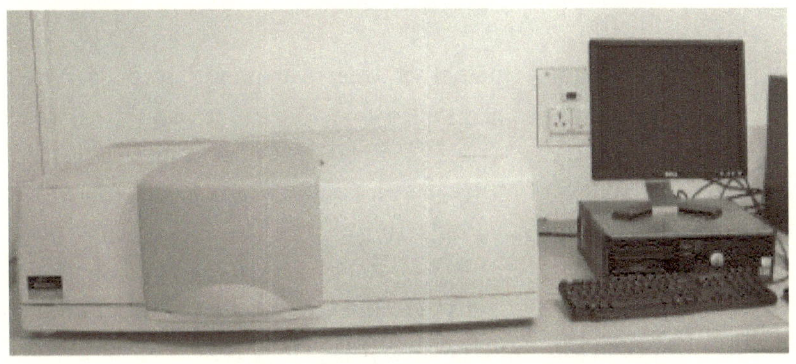

Fig. 2.2: Photograph of Jasco V670 UV-Vis-NIR spectrophotometer.

Certain technical specifications UV-Vis-NIR spectrophotometer is as follows:

The main principal of this instrument is to control the spectrophotometer with a

personal computer. It is a double beam spectrophotometer. It as SiO_2 coated reflecting

optical system with1440 lines/mm holographic grating. The spectrophotometer contains

effective photomultiplier R6872 detector for UV-Vis region and Peltier cooled PbS

detector for NIR regions respectively. Tungsten halogen and deuterium lamps are used as

source for the wavelength range 195-2500 nm.

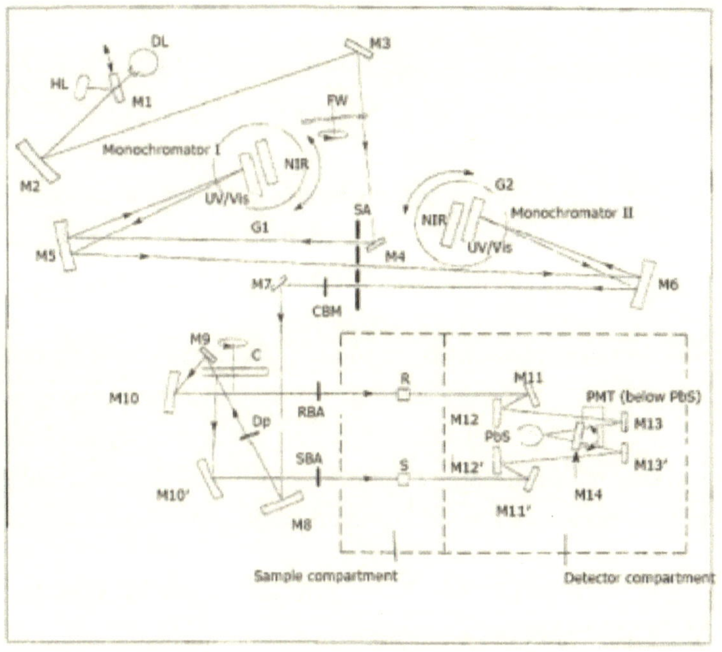

Fig. 2.3: Optical layout of Jasco V670 UV-Vis-NIR spectrophotometer.

The absorption spectra of all the rare earth - RE^{3+}-doped Cd-Zn phosphate glasses were recorded by using Jasco V670 UV-Vis-NIR spectrophotometer in the UV-Vis-NIR regions. Specifications of the spectrophotometer are shown in Table 2.1. The photograph of the block diagram and instrument are shown in Fig. 2.2 and Fig. 2.3 respectively.

The working of the mirrors and detectors and changing of wavelengths from higher to lower side and the detecting abilities are very efficient and the total mechanism of working within the spectrophotometer is well explained [a] in the instrument supplier source.

2.6. EXCITATION AND EMISSION MEASUREMENTS

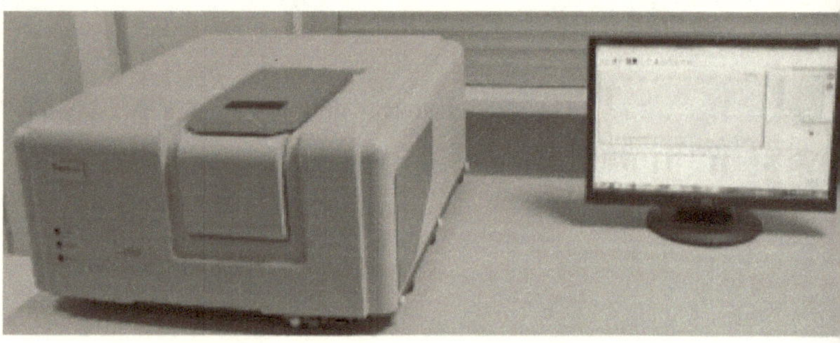

Fig. 2.4: Thermo Lumina Flourescence spectrophotometer (200-900nm)

Thermo lumina fluorescence spectrophotometer have a specific features like

High-resolution monochromators for high resolution measurements with 0.5 nm bandwidth and have the variable spectral bandwidth facility. As a source, 150 W Xenon lamp has been used for getting the full wavelength range from 190 nm to 900 nm. The spectrophotometer is designed with Customizable filters for blocking excitation and

39 | P a g

scattered light and to get highest spectral purity. The instrument is enabled with high sensitive detector for the measurements are accurate.

The above advanced specifications make an advantageous recording of specimens. For the present luminescent spectral investigations on Cd-Zn glasses excitation and emission spectra were recorded at desired wavelengths in the visible region.

2.7. FOURIER TRANSFORM INFRARED SPECTRA

Fourier transform infrared (FTIR) is the most preferred method of infrared spectroscopy to know the molecular symmetries. By passing IR radiation through a sample, some radiation is absorbed and some passes through (is transmitted) the sample. It results the molecular 'fingerprint' of the sample. With this we can identify the spectral information of new kind of composite chemicals [7].

There are four major sampling techniques in FTIR:

- Attenuated Total Reflection (ATR)

- Transmission

- Diffuse Reflectance

- Specular Reflection

Each technique has both strengths and weaknesses. In general most commonly used method is Transmission/ATR techniques based on sample phase. The working diagram is as follows:

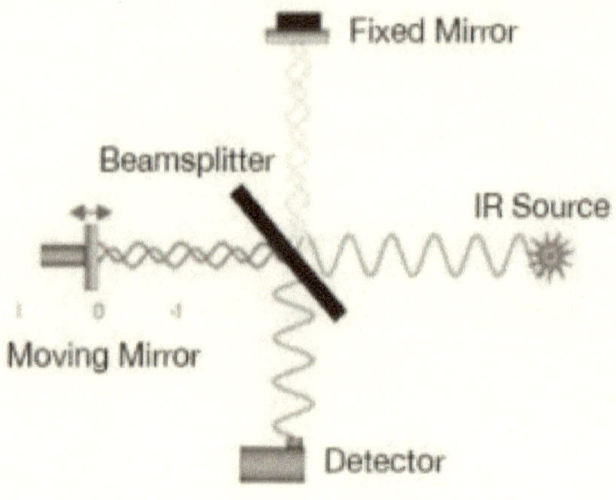

Fig 2.5: Working diagram for FTIR technique

The IR transmission spectra of these glasses in KBr matrices were recorded in the range 400-4000 cm^{-1} using BRUKER - FT / IR Fourier Transform Infrared Spectrometer.

References:

[1] https://www.shimadzu.com/an/products/ elemental-analysis/x-raydiffraction/labx-[1]   xrd-6100/ index.html

[2]   https://www.ssi.shimadzu.com/products/x-ray/ xrd-6100-7000.html[2]

[3] https://www.ursinus.ed/academics/chemistry/facilities[3] and laboratories/ instrumental-laboratory/jasco-v-670-uv-vis-nir-molecularabsorption spectrometer/

[4]   https://www.chem.uci.edu/~dmitryf/manuals/ Instructions/Jasco%20V-[4] 670%20instructions.pdf

[5]   https://www.jasco.de/en/content/ V-670/~nm.13~nc.407/V-670-UV-VIS-[5]

NIRSpectrophotometer.html

[6]   https://www.selectscience.net/products/lumina[6] fluorescence spectrometer/?prod ID=85503#tab-2

[7]   https://www.thermofisher.com/in/en/home/ industrial/spectroscopy-elemental[7]   isotope-analysis/

1. http://www.shimadzu.com/an/products/elemental-analysis/x-raydiffraction/labx-

2. http://www.ssi.shimadzu.com/products/x-ray/xrd-6100-7000.html

3. http://www.ursinus.ed/academics/chemistry/facilities

4. http://www.chem.uci.edu/%7Edmitryf/manuals/Instructions/Jasco%20V-

5. http://www.jasco.de/en/content/V-670/%7Enm.13%7Enc.407/V-670-UV-VIS-

6. http://www.selectscience.net/products/lumina

spectroscopy - elemental - isotope - analysis - learning center/ molecular - spectroscopy-information/ ftir-information/ftir-basics.html

7. http://www.thermofisher.com/in/en/home/industrial/spectroscopy-elemental

******

******

Chapter 3

Investigation on Dy^{3+} doped Metal Fluoro Phosphate glasses: Optical Studies

---

In preparation of white light generation devices, glasses doped with rare earth ions have a proper importance. In view of that, Dy^{3+} doped metal Fluorophosphate glasses were prepared and characterized with different optical studies to be useful for manufacturing of white light emission devices.

3.1 Introduction

Phosphate glasses are the prominent materials in various optical applications. Further, multicomponent Phosphate glasses have great potential. Rare earth doped Phosphate glasses with high transparency and refractive index and useful for Lasers and display devices manufacturing. In addition, Phosphate glasses have chemical durability and high gain. These Phosphate host had the feasibility to accept number of other components into the network [1-5]. Dy^{3+} ($4f^9$) ion emits infrared radiation in addition to visible light. This is very important for communication applications [6, 7]. The $^4F_{9/2}$ state is the metastable state and gives the radiative transitions upon proper excitation in visible region. It also depends on its concentration levels [8].

Dy^{3+} ions had to strong emissions in blue and yellow regions. A low intensed light [9-12] with proper excitation.

More over Dy^{3+} has excitation levels in between 340- 480 nm. These levels have potential as additional excitation source with commercially available UV and blue LED's. In order to enhance the luminescence efficiency, proper host with proper concentration of dopes ions needed. In view of that, metal Fluoro

Phosphate host was selected for this current studies because of their prominent optical properties [13-14] to cover both regions.

In this present work, using melt quenching method, transparent Dy^{3+} ions doped metal Fluoro Phosphate glasses were prepared. Optical absorption and photo luminescence activities are reported.

3.2 Materials and Methods

The following composition used to prepare the Dy^{3+} doped Cd-Pb-Na fluoro phosphate glasses. All the concentrations were taken in molar ratios.

(60-x) P2O5 – 10CdF2 – 15PbF2 – 15NaF2 – x Dy2O3 where x= 0.1, 0.3 and 0.5

(referred as P1, P2, P3 and MP4 –MgO added sample respectively).

The Glass Composition in expansion form as

59.9 P2O5 – 10CdF2 – 15PbF2 – 15NaF2 – 0.1 Dy2O3

59.7 P2O5 – 10CdF2 – 15PbF2 – 15NaF2 – 0.3 Dy2O3

59.5 P2O5 – 10CdF2 – 15PbF2 – 15NaF2 – 0.5 Dy2O3

58.5 P2O5 – 10CdF2 – 15PbF2 – 15NaF2 – 0.5 Dy2O3 +1MgO

Here after the Glass Samples are notified as P1, P2, P3 and MP4 for easy identification and representation. Total batch composition maintained 15g each and was mixed gently in an Agate mortar. Melt quenching method was use to prepare the glasses. So, the mixture was taken into a porcelain crucible and kept it into a high temperature Muffle furnace.

Its temperature was maintained and heated at 1050^0C for 1.5 hours. The molten form was quenched to room temperature and poured on a pre heated brass plate. Annelation was done for these samples at 250 $^\circ$C for about 4 hours. This kind processes removes the sudden breaks or cracks which arises due to thermal strains. The resultant samples were polished and characterized with different techniques. Density and refractive index also measured for all the samples. Optical absorption was done with JASCO V-670 Spectrophotometer. Photo luminescence spectra were recorded by using Thermo Lumina Fluorescence Spectrophotometer (200-900nm). All the recordings were done at room temperature and the excitation source is Xenon lamp.

3.3 Results and Discussions

X – Ray diffraction pattern of only P4 sample is shown in Fig.3.1. All there spectra are similar. It confirms that, there is no such sharp peaks were observed. Therefore, the prepared Cd-Pb-Na fluoro phosphate glasses were clearly amourphous in nature.

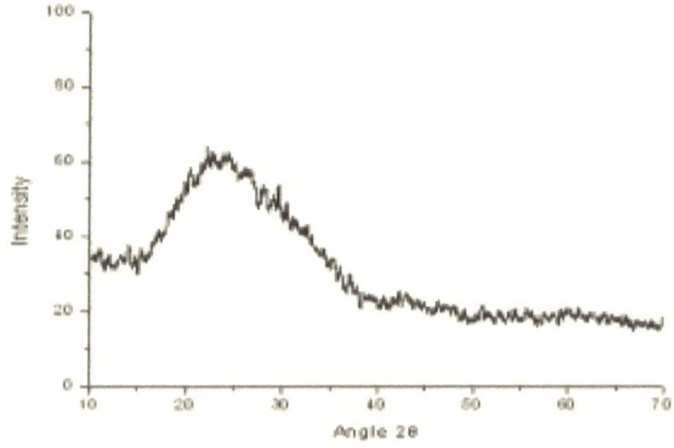

Fig.3.1: XRD pattern image of P4 glass

Fig.3.2 and Fig.3.3 shows optical absorption spectrum of all the samples in different regions. The spectra are in range 300 – 1800 nm at room temperature. In UV- Vis region, complex spectrum was observed and unable to either identify or assign the band positions for the absorption bands because of complexity in different $^{2S+1}L_J$ levels. So, the intensed infrared absorption peaks were analyzed for the Dy^{3+} ions.

All the bands exhibited by the absorption spectra were taken with their barry center and assigned to the transitions from ground state $^6H_{15/2}$ to different excited states. The band positions and the transitions are - $^6P_{7/2}$ (349 nm), - $(^4M_{19/2}+^4D_{3/2}+^6P_{5/2})$ (363 nm), - $(^4M_{21/2}+^4K_{17/2}+^4F_{7/2}+^4I_{13/2})$ (385 nm), - $^4F_{9/2}$ (452 nm in visible region. In the infrared region the band positions and the corresponding transitions are – $^6F_{5/2}$ (802 nm),

– $^6F_{7/2}$ (902 nm), – $(^6F_{9/2}+^6H_{7/2})$ (1096 nm), - $(^6F_{11/2}+^6H_{9/2})$ (1277 nm), -$^6H_{11/2}$ (1683 nm)

respectively. Here, the bands at 385 nm and 452 nm are weak in intensity. This is because, in the ultraviolet region there is a powerful absorption of network exists [16]. Judd-OFelt (J-O) parameters which signify the spectral intensities were evaluated and presented in Table - 3.1. It is well known, that the covalency nature as well as coordination environment of the dopant ions will be determined by the three important J-

O intensity parameters O2, O4 and O6. O2 parameter characterize Dy-O covalency; and

O4 and O6 correspond to the relation between Dy^{3+} ions and ligand ions.

Table-3.1, clearly shows trend $\Omega2>\Omega6>\Omega4$ for the host glass matrix. The higher the value (1.29×10^{-21}) for MP4 sample indicates higher asymmetry of crystal fied at the Dy3+ ions site. Lower asymmetry of the crystal field for P2 sample exists because of its low value (0.84×10^{-21}). So, compared to other glasses, MP4 glass had high covalency and asymmetry. Further, these parameters determines different other properties like dielectric nature, rigidity and viscosity of the host glass matrix.

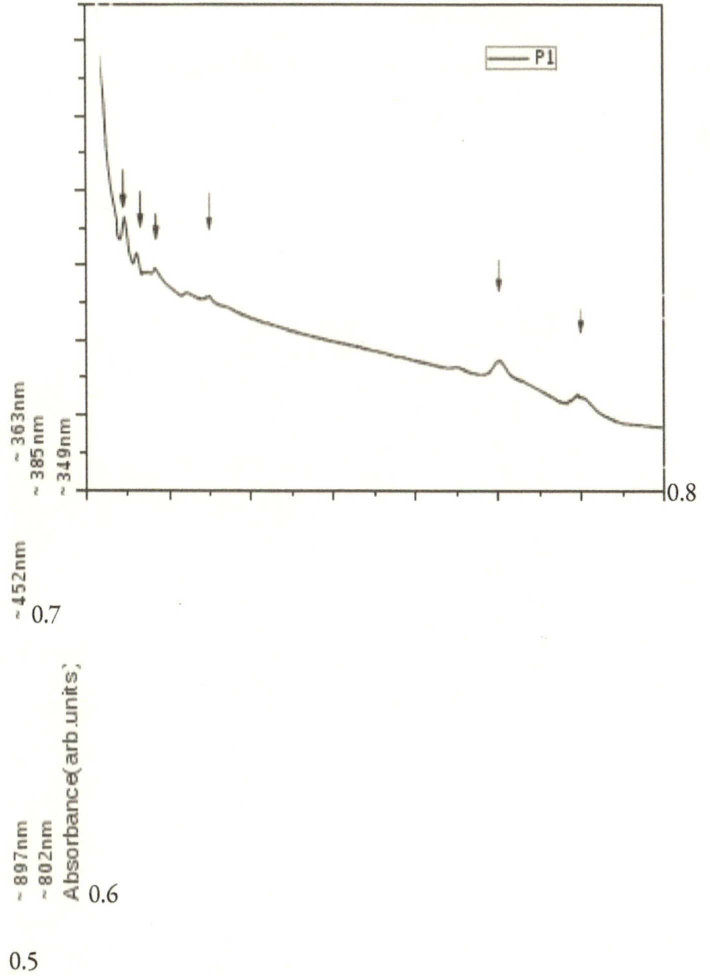
P1
~ 363nm
~ 385 nm
~ 349nm
~ 452nm
0.7
~ 897nm
~ 802nm
Absorbance(arb.units)
0.6
0.5
0.4
0.3
0.2
0.8
300 400 500 600 700 800 900 1000
Wavelength (nm)

Fig.3.2a: P1 glass absorption spectrum (Visible region)

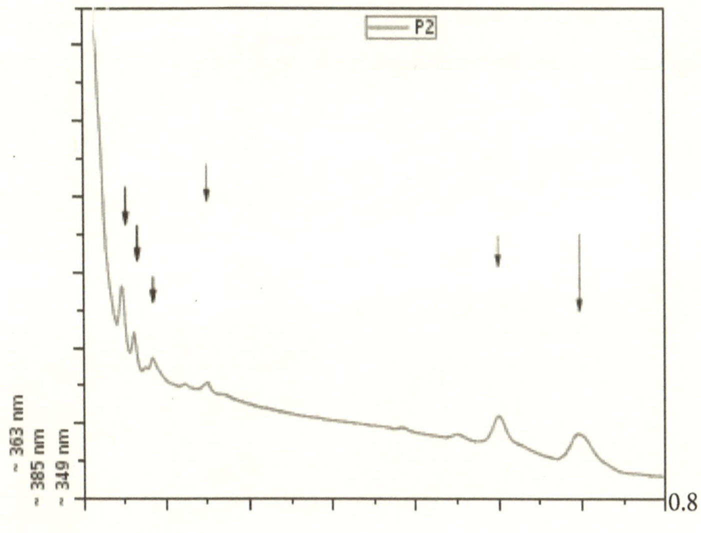
P2
≈ 363 nm
≈ 385 nm
≈ 349 nm
≈ 452 nm
≈ 897 nm
≈ 802 nm
Absorbance (arb. units)
0.8
0.7
0.6
0.5
0.4
0.3
0.2
300 400 500 600 700 800 900 1000
Wavelength (nm)

Fig.3.2b: P2 glass absorption spectrum (Visible region)

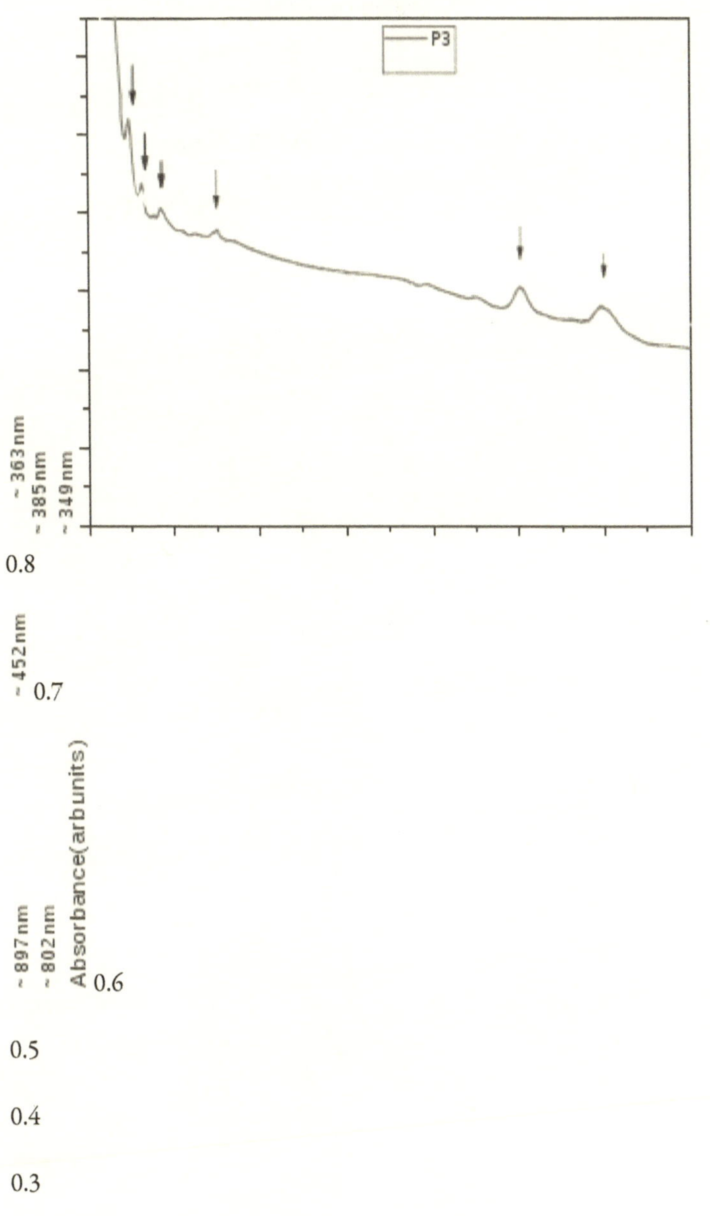
P3
~ 363 nm
~ 385 nm
~ 349 nm
~ 452 nm
~ 897 nm
~ 802 nm
Absorbance(arb units)
0.8
0.7
0.6
0.5
0.4
0.3
0.2
300 400 500 600 700 800 900 1000

Wavelength (nm)

Fig.3.2c: P3 glass absorption spectrum (Visible region)

Fig.3.2c: P3 glass absorption spectrum (Visible region)

4 | P a g e

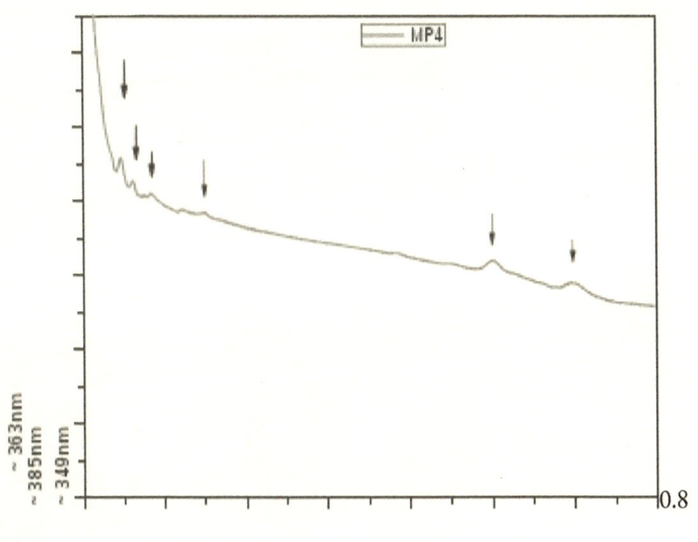

MP4
≈ 363nm
≈ 385nm
≈ 349nm
≈ 452nm
0.7
≈ 897nm
≈ 802nm
Absorbance(arb units)
0.6
0.5
0.4
0.3
0.2
0.8
300 400 500 600 700 800 900 1000
Wavelength (nm)

Fig.3.2d: MP4 glass absorption spectrum (Visible region)

Table-3.1: J-O intensity parameters for the present Cd-Pb-Nafluoro phosphate glasses

Glass	Ω_2 x10-21	Ω_4 x10-21	Ω_6 x10-21	Trend observed	Reference
P1	1.03	0.113	0.17	$\Omega_2>\Omega_6>\Omega_4$	Present Work
P2	0.89	0.05	0.162	$\Omega_2>\Omega_6>\Omega_4$	Present Work
P3	1.29	0.542	0.547	$\Omega_2>\Omega_6>\Omega_4$	Present Work
MP4	1.23	0.329	0.621	$\Omega_2>\Omega_6>\Omega_4$	Present Work
Phosphate glass	9.72	3.08	1.66	$\Omega_2>\Omega_4>\Omega_6$	[17]
ZnP glass	2.23	0.14	0.41	$\Omega_2>\Omega_6>\Omega_4$	[18]
PPbZdy	4.63	0.77	0.79	$\Omega_2>\Omega_6>\Omega_4$	[19]
SrZnPbPD10	2.15	0.04	0.82	$\Omega_2>\Omega_6>\Omega_4$	[20]

 G. CHANDANA

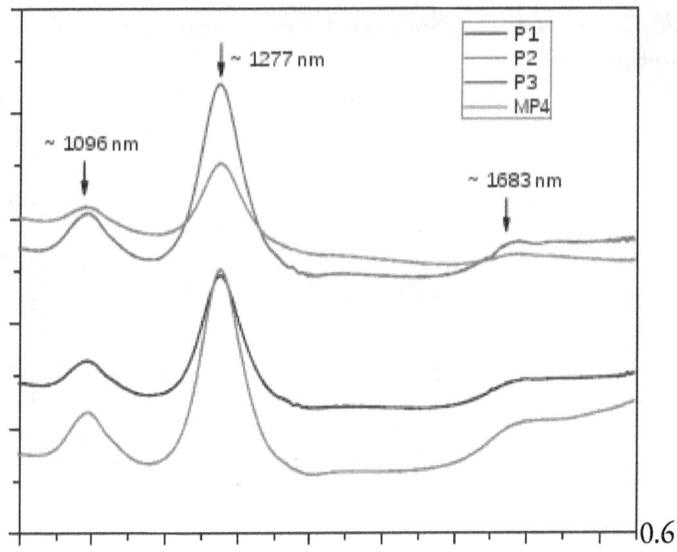

0.5

0.4

0.3

Fig. 3.3: Metal Fluoro Phosphate Glasses absoption spectra (NIR region)

To understand the excitation and emission mechanisms photoluminescence spectra were recorded for Cd-Pb-Na fluoro phosphate glasses.

Fig.3.4 shows excitation spectra and the transition corresponding to $^6P_{7/2}$ at 348 nm is prominent. This is opted as excitation wavelength for emission recording. The emission spectra is shown in Fig. 3.5. The spectra in the range of 400 – 700 nm. It shows the emission lines from the level $^4F_{9/2}$ level to the ground ^6H_J (J = 11/2, 13/2 and 15/2) in multiplets in visible region. The transitions $^4F_{9/2}\rightarrow{}^6H_{15/2}$, $^4F_{9/2}\rightarrow{}^6H_{13/2}$ and $^4F_{9/2}\rightarrow{}^6H_{11/2}$ are related to blue. (observed at ~473 nm), yellow (at ~573 nm) and red (at ~663 nm) regions. Here in red region, the emission is feeble and the others are prominent. Overall, the emission light can be white light.

Though all the glasses exhibiting white light and following the trend in intensities as MP4>P2>P1>P3. The CIE chromaticity coordinates were calculated using emission spectra. The coordinates obtained are (x,y) = (0.39,0.36) for P1; (0.28,0.33) for P2; (0.36,0.35) for P3 and (0.30,0.33) for MP4 respectively. All the coordinates were well situated in white light region. The CIE chromaticity diagram for the present glass system is shown in Fig. 3.6.

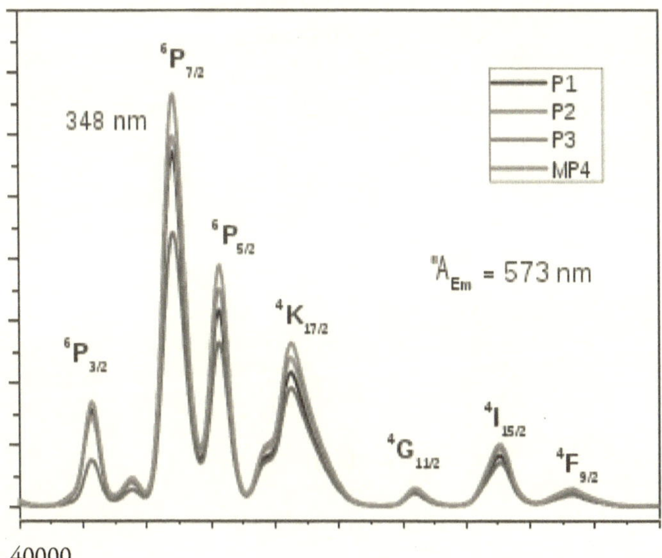

40000

35000

30000

25000

20000

15000

10000

5000

0

300 320 340 360 380 400 420 440 460 480 500
Wavelength (nm)

Fig.3.4: Metal Fluoro Phosphate Glasses - Excitation spectra (Visible region)

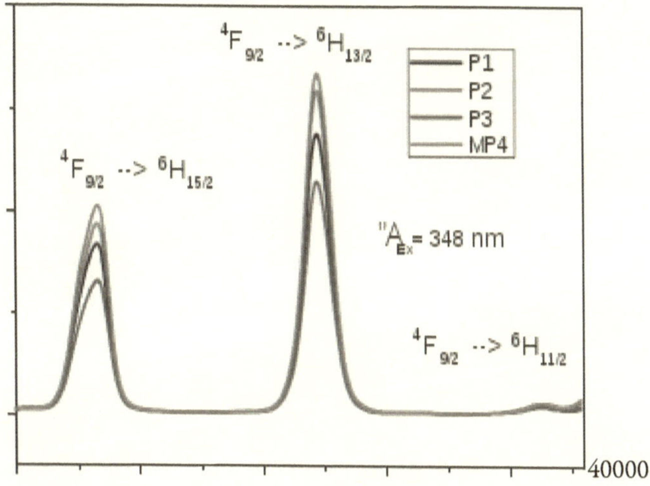
$^4F_{9/2}$ --> $^6H_{13/2}$
$^4F_{9/2}$ --> $^6H_{15/2}$
P1
P2
P3
MP4
"A_{Ex}= 348 nm
$^4F_{9/2}$ --> $^6H_{11/2}$
40000

Intensity (arb units)

20000

0

450 500 550 600 650

Wavelength (nm)

Fig.3.5: Metal Fluoro Phosphate Glasses – Emission spectra (Visible region)

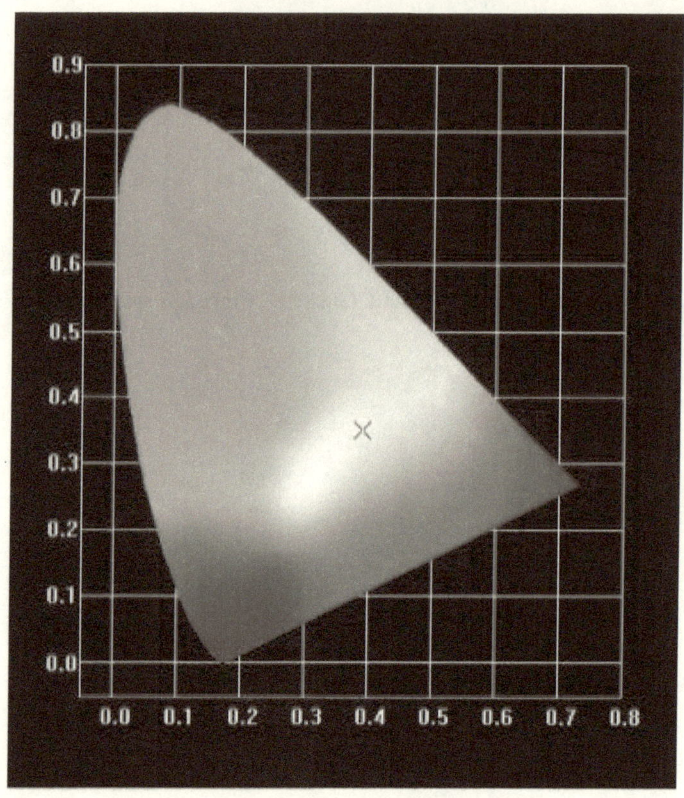

Fig.3.6: CIE Chromaticity diagram - **Cd-Pb-Na** fluoro phosphate glasses activated with Dy^{3+}

3.4. CONCLUSIONS

Metal fluorophosphates glasses (Cd-Pb-Na) doped with Dy^{3+} ions were prepared successfully by using melt quenching method. Optical absorption spectra illustrates the characterstic features of Dy^{3+} ions in the present host. Judd-Ofelt theory was used to analyze the absorption spectra and discussed the various transitions. The transitions are well in agreement with theoretical and experimental values.

The Y/B ratios of Dy^{3+} doped Cd-Pb-Na fluoro phosphates glasses are in the white light range. The chromaticity colour coordinates are well placed. All the coordinates in white light region. Therefore, the prepared metal fluoro phosphate glasses doped with Dy^{3+} ions are useful for manufacturing of white light emission devices and as well as optical applications. The presence of MgO, the emission intensity is very high with no linearity condition in concentration. The influence of MgO is also prominent and the emission intensity is in trend as MP4 > P2 > P1 > P3. So MgO playing the role of both intermediate and modifier in the present phosphate glass network.

References

[1] J.H. Campbell and T.I. Suratwala, *J. Non-Cryst. Solids.*, **263–264,** 318 (2002).

[2] S. Jiang, T. Luo, M. Myers, J. Myers, J. Lucas and N. Peyghambariam, *Proc. SPIE,* **3280,** 2 (1998).

[3] D.K. Sardar, J.B. Gruber, B. Zandi, J.A. Hutchinson and C.W. Trussell, *J. Appl. Phys.,* **93,** 2041 (2003).

[4] V. Simon, D. Muresan, A.F. Takaes, M. Neumann and S. Simon, *Solid State Ion.,*

178, 221 (2007).

[5] S. Surendra Babu, P. Babu, C.K. Jayasankar, W. Sievers, Th. Tröster and G. Wortmann, *J. Lumin.,* **126,** 109 (2007).

[6] M.L. Pang, W.Y. Shen and J. Lin, *J. Appl. Physics,* **97,** 033511(2005).

[7] N. S. Singh, R.S. Ningthoujam, N. Yaiphaba, S. Dorendrajit Singh and R.K. Vatsa, *J. Appl. Physics,* **105,** 064303 (2009).

[8] Syam Sarkar, Chanchal Hazra, Manjunath Chatti, Vasanthakumaran Sudarsan and Venkataramanan Mahalingam, *RSC Adv.*, **2,** 8269-8272 (2012).

[9] W. Wang, P. Yang S. Gai, N. Niu, F. He and J. Lin, *J. Nanopart. Res.,* **12,** 2295 (2010).

[10] P. Dimple Dutta, V. Sudarsan P. Srinivasu, A. Vinu and A. K. Tyagi, *J. Phys Chem. C*, **112**, 6781 (2008).

[11] W. Lu, H. Zhou, G.Chen, . Li, Z. Zhu, Z. You and C. Tu, *J. Phys Chem C,* **113**, 3844 (2009).

[12] C. Cao, H. K. Yang, J.W. Chung, B.K. Moon, B.C. Choi, J.H. Jeong and K. H. Kim, *J. Am. Ceram. Soc.,***94**, 3405-3411 (2011).

[13] S.V.J. Lakshman and Y.C. Ratnakaram, *Phys. Chem. Glasses,***29**, 26 (1988).

[14] B. Viana, M. Palazzi and O. LeFol, *J. Non-Cryst, Solids*, **215**, 96 (1997).

[15] S. Jiang, T. Luo, B.C.Hwang, F. Smekatala, K. Seneschal, J. Lucas and N. Peyghambarian, *J. Non-Cryst, Solids,***263-264,** 364 (2000).

[16] R. Praveena, R. Vijaya and C.K. Jayasankar, *Spectrochimica Acta Part A,***70,** 577- 586 (2008).

[17] S.P. Jamison and R.J. Reeves, *Phys. Rev. B,***67**, 115110 (2003).

[18] V. Reddy Prasad, S. Babu and Y.C. Ratnakaram, *Ind. J. Phys,***90 (10)**, 1173-1182 (2016).

[19] R. J. Amjad, M. R. Sahar S.K. Ghoshal, M. R. Dousti and R. Arifin, *Opt. Mater,*

35, 1103 (2013).

[20] V. Ravikumar, G. Giridhar and N. Veeraiah, *Luminescence* **32,** 71-77 (2017).

******

Chapter 4

Luminescence investigations on Sm^{3+} doped Cd-Pb-Na fluoro phosphate glasses

---

4.1. Introduction

Spectroscopic investigations play key role in elucidating various radiative properties of lanthanide doped glass materials along with its energy level structure and other properties [1]. Such materials are useful for LED's, next generation lighting applications, upconversion luminescent materials and optical filters [2]. Due to the long lifetimes of 4f-4f transitions and sharp spectral width, rare earth doped materials had much attractive [3]. Phosphate glasses has distinctive features like thermal stability, low melting point, high transparency, high gain density owing to high solubility for rare earth ions, low dispersion and low refractive index. In current research of solid state lighting technology, UV LED pumped glasses have much attention. In particular, for glasses doped with double, triple rare earth ions, such phosphate hosts plays important role and facilitates the doped ions to exhibit their characteristic features at higher levels. Further, the other metal fluoride component not only strengthens the network but also enhances the luminescence efficiency rare earth ions. The earlier investigations also reveals that these metal fluoride components makes the host as mechanical and chemical stable besides enhancing thermal and optical properties [2].

Among rare earth ions, trivalent Sm^{3+} ions exhibit strong reddish-orange

$(^4G_{5/2} \rightarrow {}^6H_{9/2})$ luminescence. In many host glasses like phosphate [4,5], borate [6], fluoroborates, fluorophosphates and so on [7–10], Sm^{3+} are very important and useful as an optical activator. Luminescence studies on Sm^{3+} ions in different hosts are reported well in literature. But still, it is needed to know about the internal mechanism of the host glass matrix and its structural dependency on luminescent centre. Sm^{3+} doped bismuth phosphate glasses reveals that the concentration variation of heavy metal oxide causes the structural change. Higher concentration of Sm^{3+} in the host reduced its luminescence emission due to concentration quenching. The glass host was optimized for efficient photonic materials [11]. Therefore, previous works determines the efficiency of Sm^{3+} ions in different hosts for photonic applications. Further, the Sm^{3+} doped glasses/phosphors are also using for white light generation material besides red emitting lasers and photonic applications [12–14]. However, among all the hosts fluorophosphates have much attractive and excellent with high solubility of rare earth ions, wide transmission, high thermal expansion coefficient and perfect glass forming ability [15,16].

Our work aims to explore the emission mechanism of Sm^{3+} ions doped metal fluoro phosphate at different dopant concentrations. In addition to that the structural variation by 1 mol% of MgO for higher concentration of dopant is also studied and compared with the results. The findings of this study could make a significant contribution in understanding the luminescence behavior of the Sm^{3+} ions in fluoride and oxyfluoride environment.

4.2. Experimental

The present metal fluoro phosphate (GSm Glasses) glasses were prepared by a well known melt quenching technique. The composition taken was (60-x) P_2O_5 –

10CdF2– 15PbF2 – 15NaF2 – x Sm2O3 where x=0.1, 0.3 and 0.5 (as GSm1, GSm3 and GSm5). Further, 1 mol% MgO added and it was named as MgSm5 accordingly P2O5 composition reduced. The compounds were weighed and taken around 15 g of each batch. All the compounds were well mixed in a mortar and melted in an electric furnace at 1050 °C for about 1.5h in a porcelain crucible. The melt was transferred to a preheated brass plate for quenching followed with annealing procedure to remove the thermal strains. The prepared glass samples were well polished, optical absorption spectra were recorded on Jasco-V670 spectrophotometer in the UV-Visible to NIR wavelength range. Excitation and Emission spctra were recorded on Thermo fluoro spectrometer in Visible region. Refractive index (n) was measured at room temperature by using an Abbe refractometer; 1-bromonapthalene was utilized as a contact liquid. The refractive indexes are 1.582, 1.601, 1.632 and 1.6 for GSm1, GSm3, GSm5 and MgSm5 respectively.

4.3. Results and discussion

The UV-Vis-NIR absorption spectra of the current Sm^{3+} doped metal phosphate glasses were recorded in the range 200-1600 nm range. Figure 4.1a and 4.1b shows the absorption spectra in both visible region (300-500nm) and NIR region (800-1600nm). The observed characteristic spectra of Sm^{3+} ions in this glass host is similar to the absorption spectra of Sm^{3+} in different glass hosts [17–22].

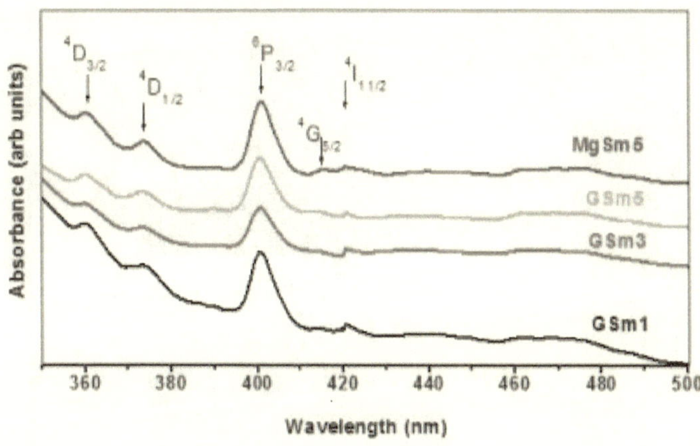

Fig 4.1: Optical absorption spectra of metal GSm glasses (UV-Vis region)

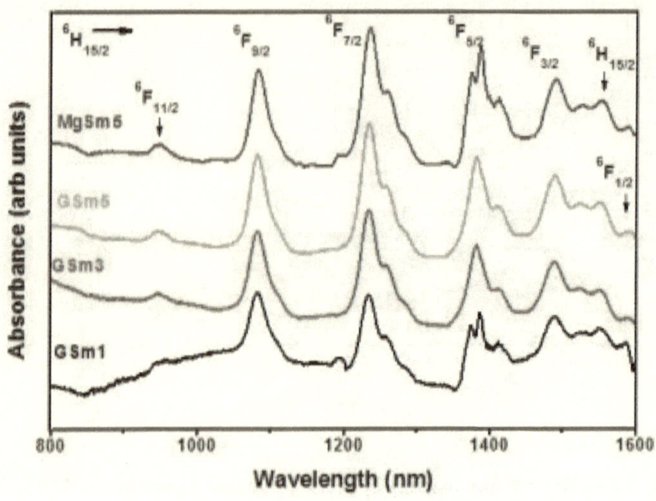

Fig 4.2: Optical absorption spectra of metal GSm glasses (NIR region)

6 | P a g e

The observed transitions are from the $^6H_{5/2}$ ground state to different excited states. These characteristic transitions of Sm^{3+} are intra-configuration (f–f) transitions. For the present study the twelve absorption bands obtained are centered at 360 nm, 373 nm, 401 nm, 413 nm, 420 nm, 949 nm, 1081 nm, 1232 nm, 1383 nm, 1486 nm, 1551 nm and 1590 nm are assigned to various transitions from ground state $^6H_{5/2}$ to excited states – $^4D_{3/2}$,

4D1/2, 6P3/2, 4G5/2,4I11/2, 6F11/2, 6F9/2, 6F7/2,

6F5/2, 6F3/2, 6H15/2 and 6F1/2 respectively

according to Carnell et al. [23].

The absorption bands of Sm^{3+} ion is separated into low energy and higher energy

groups and most of the bands were induced electric dipole transitions (1'J $\geq$ 6). Here the hypersensitive transitions $^6H_{5/2} \rightarrow {}^6F_{1/2}$ and $^6H_{5/2} \rightarrow {}^6F_{3/2}$ transitions obey the selection rules

$|\Delta S| = 0$, $|\Delta J| \leq 2$ and $|\Delta L| \leq 2$ and their shape, position and intensity are dependent on ligand coordination. The $^6H_{5/2} \rightarrow {}^6F_{7/2}$, $^4G_{5/2}$ are magnetic dipole transitions and obey the

selection rule of $\Delta J = 0, \pm 1$ [24,25].

The high intense transitions in the NIR region are spin allowed ($\Delta S = 0$) transitions. In UV region the absorption bands are feeble because of strong absorption of the prepared glass host. Here the reduction in the strength of the interelectronic repulsion due to the transfer of electron density to the bonding molecular orbitals results the increase the electron cloud around the doped rare earth ion. In other words, the bonding between lanthanide ion and ligands causes a shift in f-f transitions compared to free ion is a well known nephelauxetic effect [23].

The experimental spectral intensities were evaluated for all the observed in the absorption spectra and consequently assessed fcal[26] and Judd-Ofelt (J-O) intensity parameters($\Omega\lambda$) ; where λ=2, 4, 6) [27,28] by using least square fit method. The expressions were used from Mariappan et al. [7] to calculate the parameters. For each of the absorption transition, the calculated and experimental oscillator strength values of are presented in Table 4.1. It is noticed that both calculated and experimental oscillator strengths are in good agreement. Further, maximum f values for the $^{6}H_{5/2} \rightarrow {}^{6}F_{7/2}$ transition compared to all other transitions. The Judd-Ofelt parameters ($\Omega = 2,4,6$) are has a significance as the parameter Ω_2 is related to the both covalency of the Sm$-$O bond (strongly dependent on intensity and nature of the hypersensitive transition) [29,30] and the asymmetry of the local environment around the Sm^{3+} ions. Similarly, the Ω_4 and Ω_6 parameters are related with the bulk properties like rigidity and viscosity of the host matrix [21,22,31,32].

The evaluated Judd-Ofelt intensity parameters Ω_2, Ω_4 and Ω_6 are presented in Table 4.2 along with the reported glasses.

Table 4.1: Evaluated oscillator strengths for prepared metal fluorophosphates glasses

Transition $^6H_{5/2} \rightarrow$	GSm1 Barry centre (cm^{-1})	f_{exp}	f_{cal}	GSm3 Barry centre (cm^{-1})	f_{exp}	f_{cal}	GSm5 Barry centre (cm^{-1})	f_{exp}	f_c
$^4D_{3/2}$	27800.95	0.28	0.98	27800.95	0.25	1.28	27771.61	0.29	1
$^4D_{1/2}$	26745.12	0.27	0.07	26795.28	0.19	0.09	26788.11	0.24	0
$^6P_{3/2}$	24937.66	0.98	3.02	24962.56	0.74	3.29	24962.56	1.05	3
$^4G_{5/2}$	24137.1	-		24102.19	-		24095.22	-	
$^4I_{9/2,11/2,13/2}$	23775.56	-		23781.21	-		23737.75	-	
$^6F_{11/2}$	-		-	10579.66	0.04	0.33	10601.64	0.03	0
$^6F_{9/2}$	9254.118	1.75	1.58	9253.776	1.67	2.03	9246.161	1.83	2
$^6F_{7/2}$	8117.542	2.23	2.43	8111.682	3.27	2.99	8111.879	3.05	3
$^6F_{5/2}$	7215.007	1.86	1.49	7245.694	1.92	1.64	7241.025	2.01	1
$^6F_{3/2}$	6717.947	0.64	0.74	6722.734	0.87	0.84	6726.759	0.74	0
$^6H_{15/2}$	6434.427	0.18	0.01	6446.248	0.23	0.02	6450.656	0.34	0
$^6F_{1/2}$	6301.118	0.09	0.10	6293.345	0.08	0.15	6281.407	0.09	0
orms		±0.64			±0.82			±0.77	

Table 4.2: Judd-Ofelt parameters and their trend for the present glasses

Glass	Ω_2	Ω_4	Ω_6	Ω_4/Ω_6	Trend	Ref.
GSm1	0.32	2.8	1.78	1.57	$O_2<O_6<O_4$	Present
GSm3	0.48	2.99	2.27	1.32	$O_2<O_6<O_4$	Present
GSm5	0.32	3.08	2.21	1.39	$O_2<O_6<O_4$	Present
MgSm5	0.54	3.67	2.05	1.79	$O_2<O_6<O_4$	Present
Phosphate	1.59	8.29	4.16	1.99	$O_2<O_6<O_4$	[33]
NaPbFP	2.32	3.04	2.83	1.07	$O_2<O_6<O_4$	[34]
KPF10Sm	2.33	9.30	5.14	1.81	$O_2<O_6<O_4$	[9]
PKAPbNSm10	2.61	5.87	3.22	1.82	$O_2<O_6<O_4$	[30]
CNFB0.1S	1.092	3.007	1.462	2.06	$O_2<O_6<O_4$	[7]

NBZPSm05   0.11 4.44 4.10   1.08 $O_2 < O_6 < O_4$ [35]

NaPMg glass   0.692 5.359 3.537 1.52 $O_2 < O_6 < O_4$ [32]

PNZSm0.5   4.46 6.79 10.91 0.62 $O_2 < O_4 < O_6$ [21]

ZnMgP0.3Sm 15.1 2.71 2.5   1.08 $O_2 > O_4 > O_6$ [22]

It is observed from the table that, lower values of $\Omega 2$ suggests the local environment around the Sm^{3+} ion is nearly symmetric (lower short-range coordination impact) and the covalency of Sm-O bond is also low because of larger symmetry sites in fluoride glasses where rare earth ions well situated results low covalent bonding. Further, the magnitude of the $\Omega 4$ and $\Omega 6$ parameters was related to viscosity and rigidity; the higher values of $\Omega 4$ and $\Omega 6$ suggests that the structural network will be more open and less rigid [7] in the present glasses.

The higher values of the quality factor values also represents that, the present glass system is optically better, useful as active laser medium [22]. It is optimized GSm5 and added 1 mol % of MgO and got better results suggesting that prominent acceptability of other compounds to stabilize the network and exhibiting better emission by situating the doped Sm^{3+} ions with non non-centrometric potential. This clearly evident that the change in symmetry or inflexibility and basicity around rare earth ions not only with the concentration of rare earth ions but also with the addition of other components like network modifiers and intermediates.

Excitation and Emission spectra were recorded in the visible region for the present glass system and are shown in Figure 4.3 (Excitation spectrum of GSm5) and Figure 4.4 respectively. Excitation spectrum indicates the transitions from $^6H_{5/2}$ to different excited levels $^4D_{7/2}$, $^4D_{3/2}$, $^6P_{7/2}+^4I_{17/2}$, $^4L_{15/2}$, $^6P_{3/2}$, $(^6H,^4P)_{5/2}$, $^4G_{9/2}$ and $^4I_{11/2}$ +

$4I13/2 + {}^{4}M15/2$. Here ${}^{6}H5/2 \rightarrow {}^{6}P3/2$ (399nm) level

had the maximum absorption and is taken

as excited wavelength to record the emission spectra for the present study. Figure 4.4 shows the Emission spectra of GSm glasses exhibits Four transitions from the excited

level to different ground levels. The transitions are

${}^{4}G5/2 \rightarrow {}^{6}H5/2$ (~560 nm-greenish

yellow; magnetic dipole transition), $^4G_{5/2}{\rightarrow}^6H_{7/2}$ (~596 nm – Orange; electric dipole transition), $^4G_{5/2}{\rightarrow}^6H_{9/2}$ (~640 nm – Red; electric dipole forced transition) and $4G_{5/2}{\rightarrow}^6H_{11/2}$ (~701 nm – deep Red). The transition from $^4G_{5/2}{\rightarrow}^6H_{7/2}$ (~596 nm –

Orange) has maximum intensity in all the glass samples indicates that these samples are emitting visible orange red colour and are useful in red light emission applications. Here the electric dipole transitions are responsive for local field and magnetic dipole transitions are insensitive to the change of field around Sm^{3+} ion [11].

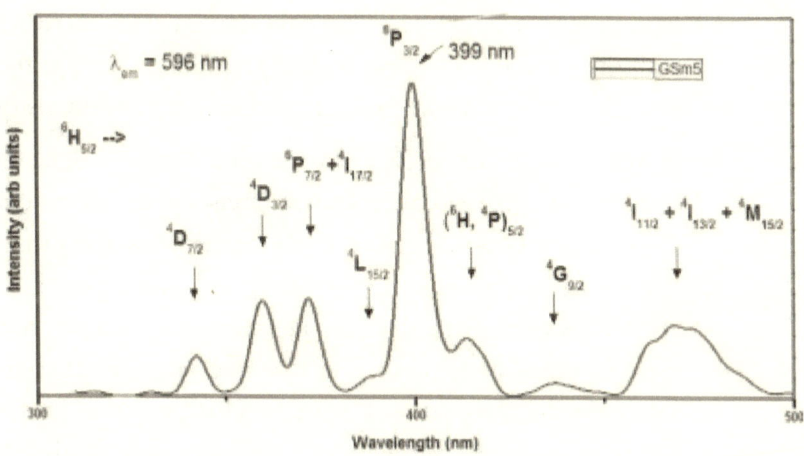

Fig 4.3: Excitation spectrum of GSm5 glass

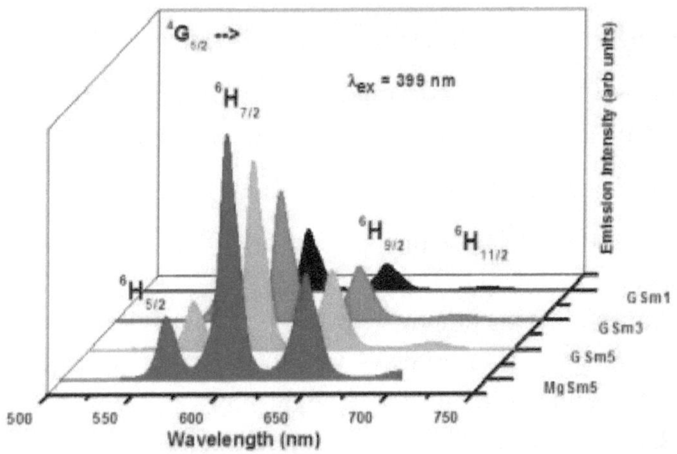

Fig 4.4: Emission spectra of GSm glass system

In the present study, for GSm5 glass has maximum luminescence intensity compared to other glasses. In many reported glasses [7,11,36], illustrates that intensity increases with the dopant concentration increases. To investigate the local field effect on enhancement of luminescence intensity of Sm^{3+} ion, in titled glasses, we added 1 mol% MgO by keeping the Sm2O3 concentration constant as 0.5 mol%. The resultant GMgSm glass shows increase in intensity than others. This small amount of MgO will participate into neither network formation nor network modification. But there is a much possibility of creating large number of defects in the glass network with MgO substitution in the cadmium sodium fluoro phosphate network leads to polycrystalline environment around Sm^{3+} ions and results in enhancement in emission intensity in all transitions. So, this study reveals that the change in local environment around Sm^{3+} ions will have a definite effect on emission properties irrespective of concentration variation of Sm^{3+} ions.

Luminescence properties such as peak emission wavelengths (λ_P), transition probability (A), branching ratios (β_{exp}) and peak emission cross-sections (σ_e) for emission transitions, $^4G_{5/2} \to ^6H_J$ (J = 5/2, 7/2, 9/2 and 11/2) were calculated and were presented in

Table 4.3. The $^4G_{5/2} \to ^6H_{7/2}$ transition in the luminescence spectra is found to have high

cross-section, branching ratio than the remaining transitions and hence high optical gain and is useful for obtaining continuous laser. Further, MgSm5 glass exhibits larger σ_e and β_{exp} values among all the prepared glasses and is optimized to be suitable for development of visible lasers and optical amplifiers. Lifetime measurements were done at room temperature and shown in Figure 4.5. Experimental and calculated lifetimes with quantum efficiencies of $^4G_{5/2}$ level for titled glasses were calculated and presented in Table 4.4.

Table 4.3: Different radiative parameters for metal fluorophosphates glasses

Transition from $^4G_{5/2} \rightarrow$	$''A_p$	GSm1			GSm3			GSm5		
		Arad	exp	a_e	Arad	exp	a_e	Arad	exp	a_e
$^6H_{5/2}$	561	72	0.23	3.27	92	0.23	3.96	91	0.24	4.09
$^6H_{7/2}$	596	168	0.55	6.74	200	0.5	7.52	202	0.54	8
$^6H_{9/2}$	643	38	0.12	1.7	74	0.18	1.81	46	0.12	2.03
$^6H_{11/2}$	703	19	0.06	1.73	24	0.06	1.67	24	0.6	1.48

Table 4.4: Experimental and calculated lifetimes of present GSm glasses

Glass	τexp	τcal	η
GSm1	2.24	3.28	68.3
GSm3	2.03	2.5	81.2
GSm5	2.28	2.69	84.7
MgSm5	2.24	2.47	90.6

One can conclude from the obtained values that MgSm5 had more efficiency (90%) than the others though lifetimes were increased as concentration increases from 64% to 84%. From the emission spectra, the calculated CIE colour coordinates for the present phosphate glasses were approximately identical with slight variation and were well placed in orange red region and is shown in Fig 4.6. The CIE coordinates (x, y) were (0.595, 0.391); (0.597, 0.386); (0.594, 0.396); (0.589, 0.387) for GSm1, GSm3, GSm5

and MgSm5 respectively. Therefore, these glasses were useful for development of orange-red lighting applications.

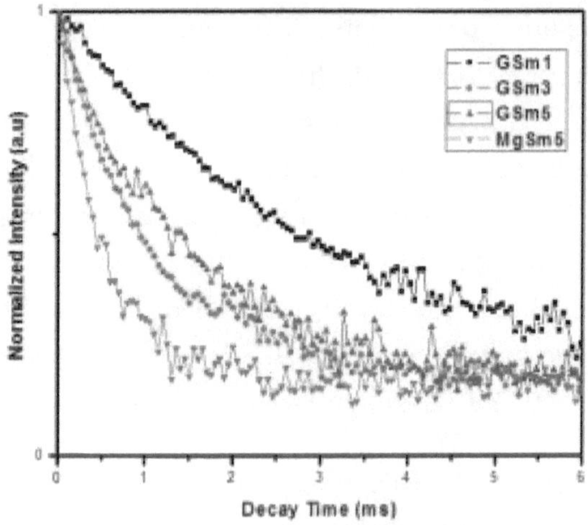

Fig 4.5: Decay profiles of prepared metal fluoro phosphate glasses

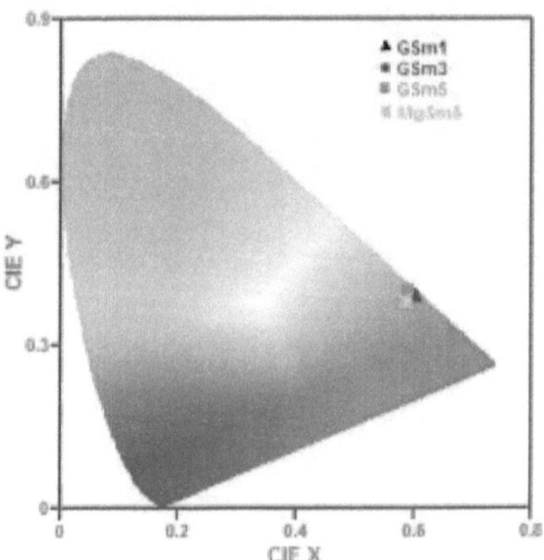

Fig 4.6: CIE chromaticity diagram showing the well placement of emission by the present Sm^{3+} doped glasses upon excitation

4.4. Conclusion

Cadmium Lead Sodium fluoro Phosphate glasses doped with Sm^{3+} ions were prepared and investigated their optical properties and established crystal field effects on Sm^{3+} ion by addition of 1mol% MgO to the composition. The evaluated J-O parameters

followed the trend as O2<O6<O4 for all the prepared glasses. The related branching ratio

and emission cross section values were higher for MgSm5 than others. The emission transitions are in visible region from $^4G_{5/2}$ state. The tranbsition $^4G_{5/2} \rightarrow {}^6H_{7/2}$ is dominant and is in red region. Overall these glasses emits orange-red colour upon excitation. By the addition of 1mol% MgO creates more defects as these atoms neither participate in network formation nor network modification. As a result, the environment around Sm^{3+} ion become more flexible for higher radiative emission in the present MgSm5 glass and is optimized. Hence these glasses were useful for preparation of Orange-Red light emitting devices.

References

[1] B. V Ratnam, M. Jayasimhadri, K. Jang, Luminescent properties of orange emissive Sm^{3+}-activated thermally stable phosphate phosphor for optical devices, Spectrochim. Acta Part A Mol. Biomol. Spectrosc. 132 (2014) 563–567.

[2] E. Pietrasik, A. Kos, M. Sołtys, W.A. Pisarski, J. Pisarska, A. Górny, Spectroscopy and energy transfer in Tb^{3+} /Sm^3+ co-doped lead borate glasses, J. Lumin. 195 (2017) 87–95. doi:10.1016/j.jlumin.2017.11.020.

[3] B.P. Singh, A.K. Parchur, R.S. Ningthoujam, P. V. Ramakrishna, S. Singh, P. Singh, S.B. Rai, R. Maalej, Enhanced up-conversion and temperature-sensing behaviour of Er^{3+} and Yb^{3+} co-doped Y2Ti2O7 by incorporation of Li^+ ions, Phys. Chem. Chem. Phys. 16 (2014) 22665–22676. doi:10.1039/C4CP02949F.

[4] Z. Mazurak, S. Bodył, R. Lisiecki, J. Gabryś-Pisarska, M. Czaja, Optical properties of Pr^{3+}, Sm^{3+} and Er^{3+} doped P2O5-CaO-SrO-BaO phosphate glass, Opt. Mater. (Amst). 32 (2010) 547–553. doi:10.1016/j.optmat.2009.11.011.

[5] Effect of ZnO on spectroscopic properties of Sm^{3+} doped zinc phosphate glasses, Phys. B Condens. Matter. 459 (2015) 79–87. doi:10.1016/j.physb.2014.11.016.

[6] R.A. Talewar, S. Mahamuda, K. Swapna, M. Venkateswarlu, A.S. Rao, Spectroscopic studies of Sm^{3+}

ions doped alkaline-earth chloro borate glasses for visible photonic applications, Mater. Res. Bull. 105 (2018) 45–54. doi:10.1016/j.materresbull.2018.04.033.

[7] M. Mariyappan, S. Arunkumar, K. Marimuthu, Concentration effect on the structural and spectroscopic investigations of Sm^{3+}ions doped B<inf>2</inf>O<inf>3</inf>–Bi<inf>2</inf>O<inf>3</inf>–C Na<inf>2</inf>O glasses, J. Lumin. 196 (2018) 151–160. doi:10.1016/j.jlumin.2017.12.026.

[8] Spectroscopic properties of Sm^{3+} ions in phosphate and fluorophosphate glasses, J. Non. Cryst. Solids. 365 (2013) 85–92. doi:10.1016/j.jnoncrysol.2013.01.030.

[9] K.A. Kumar, S. Babu, V.R. Prasad, S. Damodaraiah, Y.C. Ratnakaram, Optical response and luminescence characteristics of Sm^{3+} and Tb^{3+}/Sm^{3+} co-doped potassium-fluoro-phosphate glasses for reddish-orange lighting applications, Mater. Res. Bull. 90 (2017) 31–40.

[10] S. Thomas, R. George, M. Rathaiah, V. Venkatramu, S. Nayab rasool, N. Unnikrishnan, Structural, vibrational and dielectric studies of Sm, Physica. B.

Condens. Matter. 431 (2013) 69–74.

[11] S. Damodaraiah, V. Reddy Prasad, Y.C. Ratnakaram, Structural and luminescence properties of Sm^{3+}-doped bismuth phosphate glass for orange-red photonic applications, Luminescence. 33 (2018) 594–603. doi:10.1002/bio.3451.

[12] M.E. Alvarez-Ramos, J. Alvarado-Rivera, M.E. Zayas, U. Caldiño, J. Hernández- Paredes, Yellow to orange-reddish glass phosphors: Sm^{3+}, Tb^{3+} and Sm^{3+}/Tb^{3+} in zinc tellurite-germanate glasses, Opt. Mater. (Amst). 75 (2018) 88–93.

[13] V.K. Singh, J. Sharma, A.K. Bedyal, V. Kumar, H.C. Swart, Surface and spectral studies of Sm^{3+} doped Li4Ca (BO3)2 phosphors for white light emitting diodes, J. Alloys Compd. 738 (2018) 97–104.

[14] A.N. Meza-Rocha, S. Bordignon, A. Speghini, R. Lozada-Morales, U. Caldiño, Zinc phosphate glasses activated with $Dy^{3+}/Eu^{3+}/Sm^{3+}$ and $Tb^{3+}/Eu^{3+}/Sm^{3+}$ for reddish-orange and yellowish white phosphor applications, J. Lumin. 203 (2018) 74–82.

[15] Y. Wang, Y. Yu, Y. Zou, L. Zhang, L. Hu, D. Chen, Broadband visible luminescence in tin fluorophosphate glasses with ultra-low glass transition temperature, RSC Adv. 8 (2018) 4921–4927.

[16] K. Linganna, S. Ju, C. Basavapoornima, V. Venkatramu, C.K. Jayasankar, Luminescence and decay characteristics of

Tb^{3+}-doped fluorophosphate glasses, J. Asian Ceram. Soc. 6 (2018) 82–87.

[17] M. Seshadri, K.V. Rao, J.L. Rao, Y.C. Ratnakaram, Spectroscopic and laser properties of Sm^{3+} doped different phosphate glasses, J. Alloys Compd. 476 (2009) 263–270.

[18] J.S. Kumar, K. Pavani, T. Sasikala, A.S. Rao, N.K. Giri, S.B. Rai, L.R. Moorthy, Photoluminescence and energy transfer properties of Sm^{3+} doped CFB glasses, Solid State Sci. 13 (2011) 1548–1553.

[19] N. Deopa, B. Kumar, M.K. Sahu, P.R. Rani, A.S. Rao, Effect of Sm^{3+} ions concentration on borosilicate glasses for reddish orange luminescent device applications, J. Non. Cryst. Solids. 513 (2019) 152–158.

[20] V.R. Prasad, S. Babu, D. Rajesh, Y.C. Ratnakaram, Optical investigations of Sm^{3+} doped lead free zinc phosphate glasses, Phys. Chem. Glas. J. Glas. Sci. Technol. Part B. 56 (2015) 159–168.

[21] H. Largot, K.E. Aiadi, M. Ferid, S. Hraiech, C. Bouzidi, C. Charnay, K. Horchani- Naifer, Spectroscopic investigations of Sm^{3+} doped phosphate glasses: Judd-Ofelt analysis, Phys. B Condens. Matter. 552 (2019) 184–189.

[22] S. Hussain, R.J. Amjad, B.M. Walsh, H. Mehmood, N. Akbar, F. Alvi, M.R. Dousti, A. Sattar, A. Iqbal, S. Hussain, Calculation of Judd Ofelt parameters: Sm^{3+} ions doped in zinc magnesium phosphate glasses, Solid State Commun. (2019).

[23] W.T. Carnall, P.R. Fields, K. Rajnak, Electronic energy levels in the trivalent lanthanide aquo ions. I. Pr^{3+}, Nd^{3+}, Pm^{3+}, Sm^{3+}, Dy^{3+}, Ho^{3+}, Er^{3+}, and Tm^{3+}, J. Chem. Phys. 49 (1968) 4424–4442.

[24] K. Wang, J. Zhang, J. Wang, W. Yu, H. Zhang, Z. Wang, Z. Shao, Spectral and luminescent properties of trivalent samarium ions in $KLu(WO_4)_2$ crystals, Mater. Res. Bull. 41 (2006) 1695–1700.

[25] N.S. Hussain, V. Aruna, S. Buddhudu, Absorption and photoluminescence spectra of Sm^{3+}: $TeO_2–B_2O_3–P_2O_5–Li_2O$ glass, Mater. Res. Bull. 35 (2000) 703–709.

[26] S. Selvi, K. Marimuthu, G. Muralidharan, Structural and luminescence behavior of Sm^{3+} ions doped lead boro-telluro-phosphate glasses, J. Lumin. 159 (2015) 207–218.

[27] B.R. Judd, Optical absorption intensities of rare-earth ions, Phys. Rev. 127 (1962) 750.

[28] G.S. Ofelt, Intensities of crystal spectra of rare-earth ions, J. Chem. Phys. 37 (1962) 511–520.

[29] K.S. Lim, N. Vijaya, C.R. Kesavulu, C.K. Jayasankar, Structural and luminescence properties of Sm^{3+} ions in zinc fluorophosphate glasses, Opt. Mater. (Amst). 35 (2013) 1557–1563. doi:10.1016/j.optmat.2013.03.026.

[30] V.B. Sreedhar, C. Basavapoornima, C.K. Jayasankar, Spectroscopic and fluorescence properties of Sm^{3+}-doped zincfluorophosphate glasses, J. Rare Earths. 32 (2014) 918–926. doi:10.1016/S1002-0721(14)60163-0.

[31] V.R. Rao, C.K. Jayasankar, Spectroscopic investigations on multi-channel visible and NIR emission of Sm^{3+}-doped alkali-alkaline earth fluoro phosphate glasses, Opt. Mater. (Amst). 91 (2019) 7–16.

[32] B.N. Naick, V.R. Prasad, S. Damodaraiah, A. V Reddy, Y.C. Ratnakaram, Absorption and luminescence studies of Sm^{3+} ions activated in distinct phosphate glasses for reddish orange light applications, Opt. Mater. (Amst). 88 (2019) 7–14.

[33] G. Lakshminarayana, R. Yang, M. Mao, J. Qiu, Spectral analysis of RE^{3+} (RE= Sm, Dy, and Tm): P2O5–Al2O3–Na2O glasses, Opt. Mater. (Amst). 31 (2009) 1506–1512.

[34] S. Babu, A. Balakrishna, D. Rajesh, Y.C. Ratnakaram, Investigations on luminescence performance of Sm^{3+} ions activated in multi-component fluoro- phosphate glasses, Spectrochim. Acta Part A Mol. Biomol. Spectrosc. 122 (2014) 639–648.

[35] S. Babu, V.R. Prasad, D. Rajesh, Y.C. Ratnakaram, Luminescence properties of Dy^{3+} doped different fluoro-phosphate glasses for solid state lighting applications, J. Mol. Struct. 1080 (2015) 153–161.

[36] A. Mohan Babu, B.C. Jamalaiah, T. Sasikala, S.A. Saleem, L. Rama Moorthy, Absorption and emission spectral studies of Sm^{3+}-doped lead tungstate tellurite glasses, J. Alloys Compd. 509 (2011) 4743–4747. doi:10.1016/j.jallcom. 2011. 01.136.

******

Chapter 5

Luminescence Investigations on Pr^{3+} ions doped Metal Fluoro Phosphate glasses for Red Emission Applications

---

5.1. Introduction:

In general, to cater the needs of optical amplifiers, phosphors, upconverters, solid state lasers and transparent glass materials doped with Lanthanides (Ln^{3+}) are in great interest now a days [1,2].

Optically active ions such as transition-metal ions and/or rare-earth ions integrated glass matrix are promising candidates for luminescent systems. The rare earths in glasses induced radiative and non-radiative properties are strongly depend on composition. 4f intra- configuration of rare earth ions facilitates the dependence of structural variations on overall spectroscopic properties of the host glass due to radiative transitions. Pr^{3+} ($4f^2$) is on among the rare earth ions having simultaneous blue, green and red emissions for light and infrared (IR) emission optical amplifiers [3].

To develop the Rare earth activated optical devices, host plays a vital role with its structural convenience. Phosphate glass host is one of the important and feasible hosts for Pr^{3+}

ion because of its weak interaction among active ions. These kind of features useful for lasers and fiber amplifiers [4]. Pr^{3+} ions doped different kinds of hosts [5-13].

As all the properties of the glasses were strongly dependent on long range motions of the ions, variation in host as well as in dopant simultaneously, it is very important to understand host dependence [14].

However, the studies on simultaneous variation of host and dopant in phosphate glass are very limited. In addition to the spectroscopic investigations, it is important get the completer internal structure and the mechanism which are also responsible for the luminescence variation.

In the present investigation, the optical properties of Pr^{3+} doped cadmium lead sodium phosphate glasses with different compositions have been reported by using the Judd-Ofelt (J-O) theory [15,16] and photoluminescence spectra of these glasses.

Variation in the various properties for $^{1}D_4 \rightarrow {}^{3}H_4$ and $^{3}P_0 \rightarrow {}^{3}H_4$ emission levels of Pr^{3+} ions

in the present **(60-x) P2O5 – 10CdF2 – 15PbF2 – 15NaF2 – x Pr6O11** where x=0.1, 0.3, and 0.5 respectively (samples were named as GPr1, GPr2, GPr3 and GPr4 (MgO added)) glass system has reported as a function of compositional variation. Such that alteration of composition to be a welcome addition for the current optical technology. To the best of our knowledge work on alternative tunability of dopant concentration and modifier concentrations are very limited. This report on optical properties of the present Cd-Pb-Na fluoro phosphate glass system will be helpful to various optical and lighting applications.

5.2. Preparation and Characterization

The present glasses were prepared at a temperature range of 950-1050°C by melt quenching technique. The samples were annealed at 250°C for 4 hours to remove the thermal strains as above said and named as glass samples as GPr1, GPr2, GPr3 and GPr4 respectively. JASCO UV-Vis spectrophotometer was used to record optical absorption spectra for the polished glass samples at room temperature. Thermo fluorescence spectrometer was used to record the photoluminescence spectra. The excitation wave length, 443nm is used to excite the samples.

5.3. Results and Discussion

Room temperature absorption spectra of Pr^{3+} ions observed in G1-G15 glasses in the UV-VIS and NIR regions are same with some intensity variations and G13 sample spectra shown in Figures 5.1 and 5.2, respectively in the wavelength region 400-2500nm for good visibility of all the transitions.

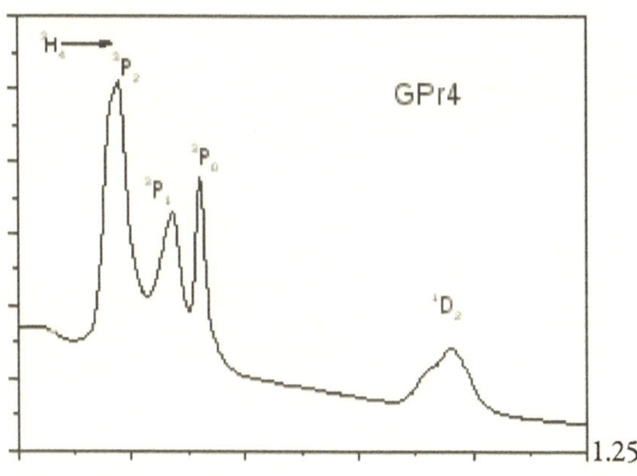

Figure 5.1: Absorption spectra UV-Vis region

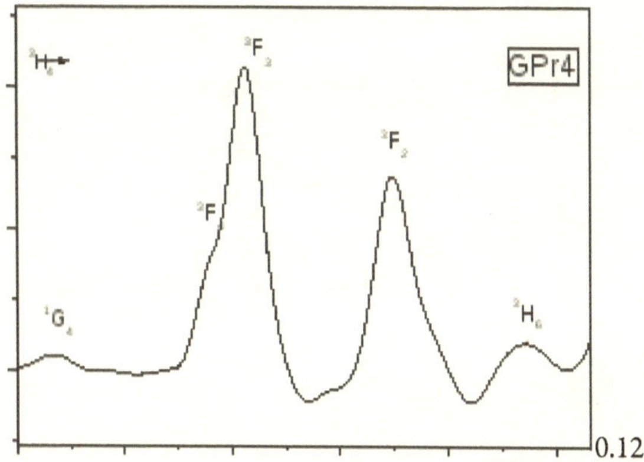

Figure 5.1(a): Absorption spectra NIR region

The observed bands from the optical absorption spectrum are at 444, 46, 480, 590, 1010, 1423, 1532 and 1950 corresponding to $^3H_4 \rightarrow {}^3P_2$, $^3H_4 \rightarrow {}^3P_1$, $^3H_4 \rightarrow {}^3P_0$, $^3H_4 \rightarrow {}^1D_2$, $^3H_4 \rightarrow {}^1G_4$, $^3H_4 \rightarrow {}^3F_4$, $^3H_4 \rightarrow {}^3F_3$, $^3H_4 \rightarrow {}^3F_2$ and $^3H_4 \rightarrow {}^3H_6$ transitions respectively for Pr^{3+}

ion [17]. Here $^3H_4$ is ground state and the remaining are excited states. The intensities may vary from host to host [14]. This is due to the presence of short range of network order in glasses. Further, the symmetry around the Pr^{3+} the Pr^{3+} ions mayvaries with in the sites. The spectrum shows that the adjacent bands overlap and appearas one. For an allowed electric dipole transition, the oscillator strengths according tothe Judd-Ofelt theory for an initial J manifold (S,L,J) and final J' manifold (S', L',J')were obtained and tabulated.

The experimental oscillator strength (measured) was calculated from the absorption spectra of glasses (Fig 1 – 3) using the expression.

$$f_{exp} = \frac{2.303 mc_2}{Nn\, e_2} \int a\,(v)\,dv = 4.318 x 10_{-9} \int a\,(v)\,dv$$

Where $\varepsilon(v)$ is the molar extinction coefficient. $\varepsilon(v)$ is obtained by the Beer – Lambart's law, expressed as

$$a\,(v) = \frac{1}{Cl}\log\frac{I_0}{I}$$

Where c-concentration of the lanthanide ion in mol/l. l-optical path length; log(I0/I) is known as absorptivity or optical density. The calculated oscillator strength was derived by Judd – Ofelt theory [15-16] is given by the expression

$$f(\backslash jJ$$

$$II\, 8n\, 2\, mcv\, l(n^2 + 2)^2\, II$$

———— ————

I I 1

cal

$$J, |jJ J) = 3h(2J+1) I 9n$$

$$Sed\,(|jJJ; |jJ J) + n\,Smd\,(|jJJ; |jJ J)\,1$$

J

All these parameters were obtained by using intermediate coupling approximation.

For Pr^{3+} ion, absorption bands, $^3F_3$ and $^3P_1$ with $^3F_4$ and $^1I_6$ were over lapped. the absorption bands were combined and treated as single experimental point.

The higher oscillator strengths in Glass represents the strong non-symmetric component of the electric field on Pr^{3+} ions.

The spectral intensities in the present explained in order to hypersensitive transitions [18, 22].

Table 5.2: Calculated J-O parameters and Quality factor

Sample Name	Ω_2	Ω_4	Ω_6	Ω_4/Ω_6
GPr1	2.487	0.098	0.343	0.285714
GPr2	3.122	0.094	0.379	0.248021
GPr3	3.669	0.104	0.480	0.216667
GPr4	4.085	0.109	0.492	0.221545

Table shows J – O parameters ($\Omega\lambda$) obtained for the three glasses by using least square fit method with the host invariant square reduced matrix elements $||U^\lambda||^2$. The lasing efficiency of prepared glasses is determined by spectroscopic quality factor (Ω_4/Ω_6) evaluated and are presented in table. It can be seen that spectroscopic quality factor is more for Glass indicates the superior quality in lasing action.

Radiative Properties

Using the J–O parameters, the radiative parameters such as branching ratio (β_r), radiative transition probability (A), total transition probability (A_T), integrated absorption cross section (σ_a) and radiative lifetimes (τ_R) have been evaluated theoretically for some of the fluorescent levels. The radiative transition probability of a fluorescent level is given by the equation [19-20].

$$64n \; {}_{4v \, 3} \, 1 \, n\left(n \, {}_2 + 2\right){}_2 \, 1$$

8 | P a g e

$$A_R\left(\backslash jJJ , \backslash jJ \, IJ \, I\right) =$$

$$3h\left(2J + 1\right) I \, 9$$

$$S\left(\backslash jJJ , \backslash jJ \, IJ \, I\right) + n \, {}_3 \, S\left(\backslash jJJ , \backslash jJ \, IJ \, I\right) 1$$

$$1J$$

Sed is the electric dipole line strength and Smd is magnetic dipole line strength of the transition. The electric dipole line strength Sed and magnetic dipole line strength is given by the equations

S_{ed}

$$(\backslash jJJ ; \backslash jJ \, IJ \, \mathrm{I}) = e\,2$$

$${}^2\mathrm{I.\,O}\ {}_{''A}\ {}^{''A\,=\,2,4,6}$$

2

$$\rangle\!\langle\!|||_{\backslash jJJ}\ U\ {}^{''A}\ \backslash jJ\ IJ\ \mathrm{I}$$

$$\frac{e^2 h^2}{16 n^2 m^2 c^2}\, k_S\,(\backslash jJ\ \backslash jJ\ \mathrm{I}\ \mathrm{I} =$$

$$\backslash jJ$$

$$+\ \backslash jJ\,\mathrm{I}\,\mathrm{I}$$

$$|||$$

$${}_{md}J\,;J\,)$$

$$JL\,2SJ$$

$\rangle\!$The three intensity parameters $O''A$ ($''A = 2,4,6$) are known as phenomenological J-O intensity parameters. In the calculation of radiative transition probability (A) the term magnetic dipole line strength Smd is neglected as the magnetic dipole mechanism have a very low spectral intensity when compared with electric dipole line strength Sed. The fluorescence branching ratio is given by the expression

$$(\backslash jJJ , \backslash jJ \, IJ \, I) = \frac{A(\backslash jJJ , \backslash jJ \, IJ \, I)}{{}_T A_R \, (\backslash jJJ)}$$

The fluorescence branching ratio is used to understand the lasing potentiality in glasses. Where AT is the total transition probability and is obtained with the formula.

$$A_T(\backslash jJJ) = \underset{\backslash jJ \, IJ \, I}{I.} \; A_R(\backslash jJJ ; \backslash jJ \, IJ \, I)$$

The above expression shows that total transition probability is obtained by summing the individual probability values.

The radiative lifetime is an effective average over site to site variation. The reciprocal of the total transition probability gives the radiative lifetime of a transition. i.e.,

---

$$T_R(\lvert jJJ) =$$

$$\cfrac{1}{A_T(\lvert jJJ)}$$

By using the J – O parameters from table and from the above equations, the transition probability rates (A), total transition probability (AT), branching ratio (βr) and radiative lifetimes (τR) have been evaluated for certain excited states. Table 5 shows the total transition probability (AT) in s^{-1}. The radiative lifetimes (τR) in μs also shown in Table 5.

The integrated absorption cross section σa is given by [21].

$$''A_4$$

$$a(\lvert jJJ, \lvert jJ \; IJ\,I) = \; _{\wp}\, A(\lvert jJJ, \lvert jJ \; IJ\,I)$$

$$_{\wp_e}\, 8n \; cn_2 \; 1''A_R$$

All the radiative properties said above for Pr^{3+} doped glasses are tabulated in table 5.3. Radiative lifetimes (τR) in μs for the fluorescent levels of Pr^{3+} ions in the present glasses have been given in table 5.3.

When comparing the J – O parameters of Pr^{3+} ions in various glasses are compared. It is interesting to note that in most cases the order of the Ωλ parameter is Ω2> Ω6>Ω4. The branching ratio and spectroscopic quality factor for all the glasses in the present system. Weber and Jacob [22] have reported that spectroscopic quality factor can be used to characterize the glasses. Stimulated emission cross sections are calculated for the observed emission transitions of Pr^{3+} for the present glasses. This cross section manifests the laser transitions.

Excitation and Emission Studies

Excitation spectrum is recorded with emission wavelength 598 nm and observed the excitation bands corresponding to $^3H_4 \rightarrow ^3P_2$, $^3P_1$ and $^3P_0$ transitions at 443, 468 and 480nm respectively and shown in Fig. 5.2. The band at 443 nm related to $^3H_4 \rightarrow ^3P_2$ transition is more intense and chosen this as excitation wavelength to record the emission spectra for present glasses.

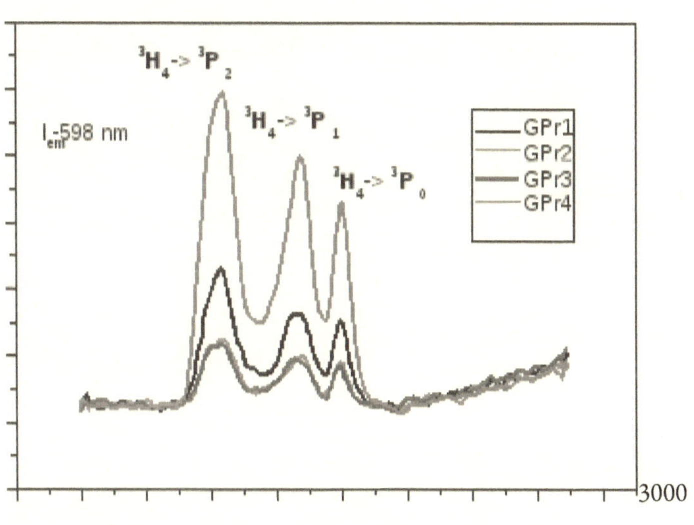

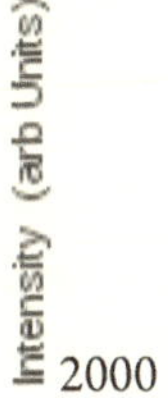

Figure 5.2: Excitation spectra of Pr^{3+} doped Cd-Pb-Na Fluoro phosphate glasses

Fig. 5.3 shows the emission spectra of Pr^{3+} in the present phosphate glasses and it contains two emission bands as one intense band and one feeble band related to

$1D2 \rightarrow {}^{3}H4$ and ${}^{3}P0 \rightarrow {}^{3}F2$ transitions respectively.

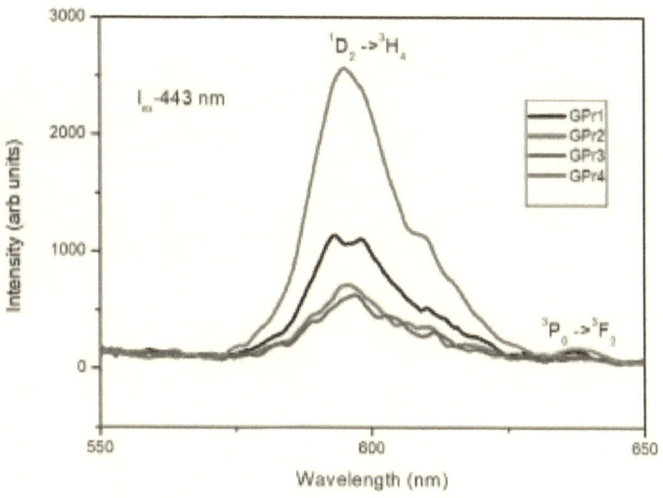

Figure 5.3: Emission spectra of Pr^{3+} doped Cd-Pb-Na Fluoro-phosphate glasses

There is a variation in profiles corresponding to modifiers but not with change in peak positions. That is intensities are varying with local environment Fig 5.4. shows the energy level diagram Pr^{3+} ions in the present glass system. Due to excitation with443 nm, emission radiations at 598 and 636 nm in cadmium phosphate glasses appears as red in colour.

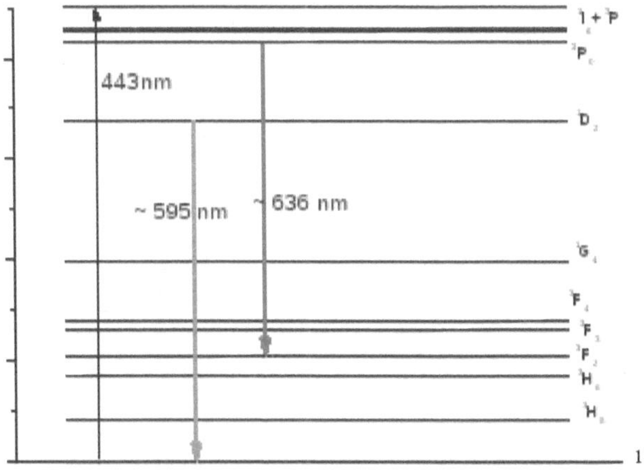

20000

15000

10000

5000

Figure 5.4: Energy level diagram for Pr^{3+} ion

Fig 5.5 shows the luminescence intensity variation as function of increase in Pr^{3+} concentration and addition of MgO.

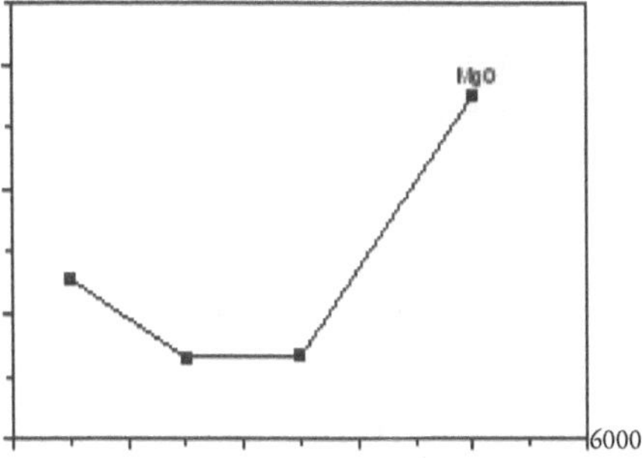

Figure 5.5: Activator concentration Vs Modifier Concentration

From fig. 5.5, luminescence intensity of Pr^{3+} ions in cadmium phosphate glass host is higher at MgO addition. In other cases there is such linear decrease occurs. This indicates the intensity dependence on local environment of host glass matrix. That is, in that particular point it shows the increasing interaction among the Pr^{3+} ions which gives an evidence of structural changes of host even at lower concentrations of luminescent centers [23].

In the present cadmium phosphate glass matrix, the structural changes are clearly in evidence with the well resolved splitting at lower wavelength (595nm) side of emission peak.

Radiative transition probabilities (Arad), peak wavelengths, peak emission cross- sections and effective line-widths for different concentrations of glass matrices are presented in Table. $^3P_0$-$^3F_2$ transition has higher emission cross section than others.

Table 5.3: Calculated radiative parameters by using J-O parameters and Emission intensities

Sample name	State/ transition	A_T	$\tau_R\%$	τ_E^P	τ_R (sec)
G1	$_3P_0 \rightarrow _3F_2$	3.58615E+22	2.78851E-23	4.25062E-08	0.000120865
	$_1D_2 \rightarrow _3H_4$	4.73996E+21	2.10972E-22	9.24608E-11	0.000182888
G2	$_3P_0 \rightarrow _3F_2$	4.46178E+22	2.24126E-23	4.93729E-08	9.71453E-05
	$_1D_2 \rightarrow _3H_4$	5.94269E+21	1.68274E-22	1.04658E-10	0.000145874
G3	$_3P_0 \rightarrow _3F_2$	9.91706E+22	1.00836E-23	5.12131E-08	4.37066E-05
	$_1D_2 \rightarrow _3H_4$	1.0061E+22	9.93939E-23	5.90784E-10	8.61627E-05
G4	$_3P_0 \rightarrow _3F_2$	5.78725E+22	1.72794E-23	7.27422E-08	7.48958E-05
	$_1D_2 \rightarrow _3H_4$	7.74532E+21	1.2911E-22	1.54795E-10	0.000111923

CIE Chromaticity Coordinates

Standard functions for the three primary colors were determined in 1931 by the Commission Internationale de l'Eclairage (CIE), the International Commission on Illumination. Tristimulus functions were derived by determining the average response of the human eye. The spectral radiance associated with the three color functions was integrated in order to specify color.

Thus,

$$X = f\, cp(A) < (A)8A \; ; \; Y = f\, cp(A)l/J(A)8A \; ;$$

Z =f cp(A)((A)8A , where x(J), y(J), z(J) are tristimulus functions. The chromaticity coordinates x, y, z, are then determined by normalizing each of the tristimulus functions

such that

x= X/(X+Y+Z) y= Y/(X+Y+Z) z= Z/(X+Y+Z) and x+y+z=1. The chromaticity diagram shown in Figure 5.2 corresponds to wavelengths of spectrally pure colors and in bounded by the reduced x and y coordinates. The three primary colors red, blue and green, can be combined to produce the entire color gamut.

The CIE coordinates of our most intense sample, were calculated using the Color calculator program. The coordinates were found to be x = 0.69, y = 0.287, which lies (as a small blue circle) on the edge of orange red and leaning strongly to red colour as shown in Figure.

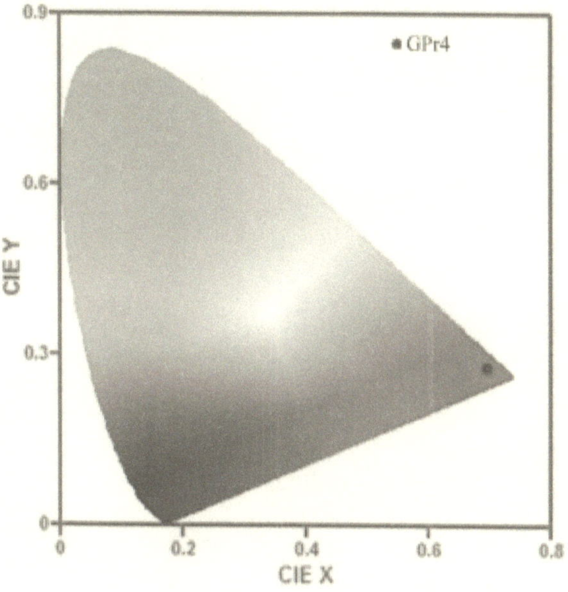

Figure 5.6: CIE diagram for Pr^{3+} doped cadmium phosphate glasses

Infrared Studies

The FTIR spectra of the rare earth doped Cadmium Lead Sodium Phosphate (Cd- Pb-Na) glasses are produced the maximum same spectra because of constant phosphate fundamental frequencies. So GPr4 sample spectrum is specified in Fig. 5.7.

G. CHANDANA

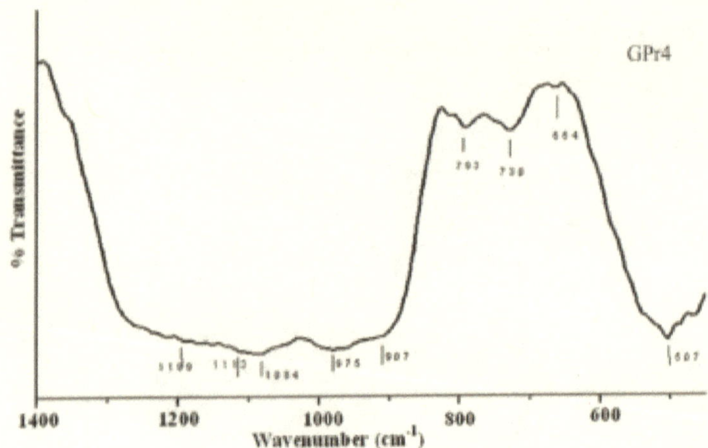

GPr4

Figure 5.7: FTIR spectra of GPr4 Cd-Pb-Na Fluoro Phosphate glass

The spectra are recorded in the range of 1400-400 cm^{-1}. The results of the FTIR spectral studies disclosed as,

⁴The phosphate units PO^{3-} may exists in the range 1400-400 cm^{-1}. The phosphate

ion in the free state exists in tetrahedral symmetry and exhibits four fundamental modes at 1082 ($v3$), 980 ($v1$), 515 ($v4$) and 363 ($v2$). Here $v1$ is non-degenerate, $v2$ is doubly degenerate and $v3$, $v4$ are triply degenerate. In this case $v3$, $v4$, only are infrared active.

Usually, there is a distortion in the ideal Td symmetry in phosphate ion and because of this, the degencracy of the infrared active vibrations ($v3$ and $v4$) were removed. In addition to that, infrared non active vibrations $v1$ and $v2$ may become visible in the infrared spectrum.

At 1082 and 980 cm^{-1} are the two fundamental vibrational frequencies of

$_4$PO^{3-}ion [24]. Further, the band at in infra red region [25] and the bands at 1100 ~ 1040 cm^{-1} only are phosphate ions bands [26].

P-O linkages of linear polyphosphates were observed earlier by Miller and Wilkins [27] and are become characteristic feature.

Characteristic absorptions near 900 and 700 cm^{-1} are related to [24] that compounds containing P-O-P links.

Symmetric stretching of P-O-P groups corresponds to two modes appearing at around 680 ~ 785 cm^{-1}. At ~ 980 cm^{-1} the absorption band represents the (PO3) symmetric stretching mode.

PO2 stretching vibrations are present ~ 1180 cm^{-1} in this cadmium phosphate

glass.

The strong bands in the region 880 ~ 910 cm^{-1} are due to P-O-P asymmetric vibration.

In the present case three bands are observed and these are identified as pertaining to v1, v3 and v4. So, from all the data of infrared spectra confirms the host glass, and supports the mixed alkali effect in these cadmium phosphate glasses.

5.4. Conclusions

➤ Hyperfine transition is not excluded from the results because of good fits in the J- O parameters.

➤ Concentration variation of oscillator strengths is clearly shown by these intensity parameters.

➤ In all the prepared glasses the J-O parameters have the values as O2>O6>O4

➤ By the excitation of 442 nm, two emission peaks were observed in the red region by the transitions from $^3P_0 \rightarrow ^3H_4$ and $^1D_2 \rightarrow ^3H_4$.

➤ From the calculated lifetimes it is observed that the present host is the good for laser applications which will be operated at the wavelength of ~ 600nm.

➤ From the FTIR spectral studies, the spectrum reveals the fundamental frequencies of phosphate units

From the above results it is concluded that the present host is suitable for sensitive red emitting lasers and fiber amplifiers with a marginal environmental changes

References:

[1] R.C. Powell, Physics of solid-state laser materials, Springer Science & Business Media, 1998.

[2] D.C. Brown, High-peak-power Nd: glass laser systems, Springer, 2013.

[3] A.A. Kaminskii, Laser Crystals, Optical Sciences, V14, (1981).

[4] Z. Mazurak, S. Bodyl, R. Lisiecki, J. Gabryś-Pisarska, M. Czaja, Optical properties of Pr^{3+}, Sm^{3+} and Er^{3+} doped P_2O_5–CaO–SrO–BaO phosphate glass, Opt. Mater. (Amst). 32 (2010) 547–553.

[5] W.T. Carnall, P.R. Fields, K. Rajnak, Spectral intensities of the trivalent lanthanides and actinides in solution. II. Pm^{3+}, Sm^{3+}, Eu^{3+}, Gd^{3+}, Tb^{3+}, Dy^{3+}, and Ho3+, J. Chem. Phys. 49 (1968) 4412–4423.

[6] Y. V Malyukin, P.N. Zhmurin, R.S. Borysov, M. Roth, N.I. Leonyuk, Spectroscopic and luminescent characteristics of PrAl3 (BO3)4 crystals, Opt. Commun. 201 (2002) 355–361.

[7] D.K. Sardar, F. Castano, Characterization of spectroscopic and laser properties of Pr^{3+} in Sr5(PO4)3F crystal, J. Appl. Phys. 91 (2002) 911–915.

[8] S. Okamoto, H. Yamamoto, Luminescent properties of praseodymium-doped alkaline-earth titanates, J. Lumin. 102 (2003) 586–589.

[9] P. Babu, C.K. Jayasankar, Spectroscopy of Pr^{3+} ions in lithium borate and lithium fluoroborate glasses, Phys. B Condens. Matter. 301 (2001) 326–340.

[10] A.B. Seddon, D. Furniss, M.S. Iovu, S.D. Shutov, N.N. Syrbu, A.M. Andriesh,

G.J. Adriaenssens, The effect of oxygen on optical absorption and emission of Pr: Ga–La–S glass, J. Non. Cryst. Solids. 326 (2003) 279–282.

[11] G. Jose, V. Thomas, Gijo Jose, PI Paulose, NV Unnikrishnan, J. Non-Cryst. Solids. 319 (2003) 89–94.

[12] H. Yamamoto, S. Okamoto, H. Kobayashi, Luminescence of rare-earth ions in perovskite-type oxides: from basic research to applications, J. Lumin. 100 (2002) 325–332.

[13] G.H. Dieke, H.M. Crosswhite, H. Crosswhite, Spectra and energy levels of rare earth ions in crystals, (1968).

[14] Y.C. Ratnakaram, D.T. Naidu, A. Vijayakumar, J.L. Rao, Studies on optical absorption and luminescence properties of Dy^{3+} doped mixed alkali borate glasses,

Opt. Mater. (Amst). 27 (2004) 409–417.

[15] B.R. Judd, Optical absorption intensities of rare-earth ions, Phys. Rev. 127 (1962) 750.

[16] G.S. Ofelt, Intensities of crystal spectra of rare-earth ions, J. Chem. Phys. 37 (1962) 511–520.

[17] L.R. Moorthy, M. Jayasimhadri, A. Radhapathy, R. Ravikumar, Lasing properties of Pr^{3+}-doped tellurofluorophosphate glasses, Mater. Chem. Phys. 93 (2005) 455– 460.

[18] J.A.M. Neto, D.W. Hewak, H. Tate, Application of a modified Judd-Ofelt theory to praseodymium-doped fluoride glasses, J. Non. Cryst. Solids. 183 (1995) 201– 207.

[19] R. Jacobs, M. Weber, Dependence of the $^{4}F_{3/2} \rightarrow {}^{4}I_{11/2}$ induced-emission cross section for Nd^{3+} on glass composition, IEEE J. Quantum Electron. 12 (1976) 102– 111.

[20] C.W. Nielson, G.F. Koster, Spectroscopic Coefficients for the pn, dn, and fn Configurations, MIT press, 1963.

[21] M. Rotenberg, R. Bivins, N. Metropolis, J.K. Wooten Jr, The Tables of 3j and 6j Symbols, (1959).

[22] D.E. McCumber, Theory of phonon-terminated optical masers, Phys. Rev. 134 (1964) A299.

[23] G. Blasse, B.C. Grabmaier, A general introduction to luminescent materials, in: Lumin. Mater., Springer, 1994: pp. 1–9.

[24] D.E.C. Corbridge, E.J. Lowe, J. chem. Soc.[London], (1954).

[25] G. Herzberg, Infrared and Raman spectra of polyatomic molecules, Krieger Publishing Company, 1945.

[26] N.B. Colthup, Spectra-structure correlations in the infra-red region, JOSA. 40 (1950) 397–400.

[27] F.A. Miller, C.H. Wilkins, Infrared spectra and characteristic frequencies of inorganic ions, Anal. Chem. 24 (1952) 1253–1294.

******

Chapter 6

Spectroscopic Investigations on UV and Laser Irradiated Dy^{3+}, Pr^{3+} and Sm^{3+} doped CdF$_2$ – PbF$_2$ – NaF$_2$ – P$_2$O$_5$ glasses for Optical applications

The work in the current chapter presents the photoluminescence behavior of current metal fluoro phosphate glasses. Rare earth ions were doped for luminescence behavior and then studied after UV and Laser irradiations [1–4]. Spectroscopic techniques like optical absorption, photoluminescence were used to study the characteristic optical behavior at room temperature. The irradiated glasses also shows the configurational behavior. Photoluminescence studies explained the light emission upon suitable excitation by these glasses. The results were compared with pure glasses and found that there is a slight enhancement in emission behavior after irradiation. The details of the complete study are as follows:

6.1 INTRODUCTION

The phosphate glasses are very important materials in optical applications. Particularly, the phosphate glasses doped with rare earth ions are in great interest forboth lighting and laser applications [5–8]. In the present case, we choose the rare earth ions doped glasses i.e., Dy^{3+}, Pr^{3+} and Sm^{3+} with 0.5 mol% concentrations doped metalfluoro phosphate glasses to investigate their luminescence behavior after UV and Laser irradiation.

It is well known that, Dy^{3+} have the transitions from meta-stable state $^4F_{9/2}$ to different lower levels $^6H_{7/2}$, $^6H_{9/2}$, $^6H_{11/2}$, $^6H_{13/2}$ and $^6H_{15/2}$ [9–11]. These transitions give photo-energies in visible region as white light. When comes to individual transitions, Dy^{3+} gives a strong emission line in yellow region belongs to $^4F_{9/2}$ to $^6H_{15/2}$.

Pr^{3+} has its own significance in preparation of many types of optical devices like up converters, optical amplifiers and optical fibers. Close energy separation is an added advantage for Pr^{3+} to prepare UV-Vis-NIR lasers [12,13]. This rare earth ion is useful in manufacturing of devices with red emission. Here, for each incident UV excitation photon will generate more than one photon by Pr^{3+} ions in solids.

Similarly, the glasses doped with Sm^{3+} ions are also much significant in fabrication of optical devices. The Sm^{3+} ion has $(4f^5)$ configuration and emits photo energy. This energy has high quantum efficiency and it's from meta stable state $^4G_{5/2}$ [14– 16]. It is useful in various applications like undersea communications, high density memory devices, colour displays and solid state lasers.

6.2 EXPERIMENTAL

Metal Fluoro Phosphate glasses with different rare earth ions were prepared. Well known glass preparation method, melt quenching was used to prepare the glasses. The molar chemical compositions are as follows:

A: 59.5 P_2O_5 – 10CdF_2 – 15PbF_2 – 15NaF_2 – 0.5Dy_2O_3 B: 59.5 P_2O_5 – 10CdF_2 – 15PbF_2 – 15NaF_2 – 0.5Pr_6O_{11} C: 59.5 P_2O_5 –

$10CdF_2 - 15PbF_2 - 15NaF_2 - 0.5Sm_2O_3$

Glasses are denoted as A,B and C; pure glasses

as UVA, UVB and UVC for UV irradiated glasses as LA, LB and LC for Laser irradiated glass.

101| P a g

Commercial UV lamp has been used for irradiation of glasses. The wavelength of the light is 254 nm. All the samples were kept for 20h under UV lamp.

Commercial 632nm RED emitting laser was used for irradiation purpose and focused on a targeted region of the glass specimens for 20h continuously. Both the irradiation processes were done at room temperature.

6.3 RESULTS AND DISCUSSIONS

6.3.1 Absorption studies of Dy^{3+} doped Irradiated glasses (UVA and LA glasses):

Ultraviolet and Laser irradiated glasses absorption spectra were recorded in the range of 300 nm –1800 nm. The spectra were shown in Fig. 6.1 and 6.2 separately. The spectra shows similar to the pure glass doped with Dy^{3+} ions. The transitions were

assigned as follows from its ground state $^6H_{15/2} \rightarrow {}^4I_{13/2},\ {}^4G_{11/2},\ {}^4I_{15/2},\ {}^4F_{9/2},\ {}^6F_{3/2},\ {}^6F_{5/2},\ {}^6F_{7/2},$

6F9/2, $^6F_{11/2}$ and $^6H_{15/2} \rightarrow {}^6H_{11/2}$ [17–19]. All the bands observed for both UV irradiated and Laser irradiated glasses were tabulated.

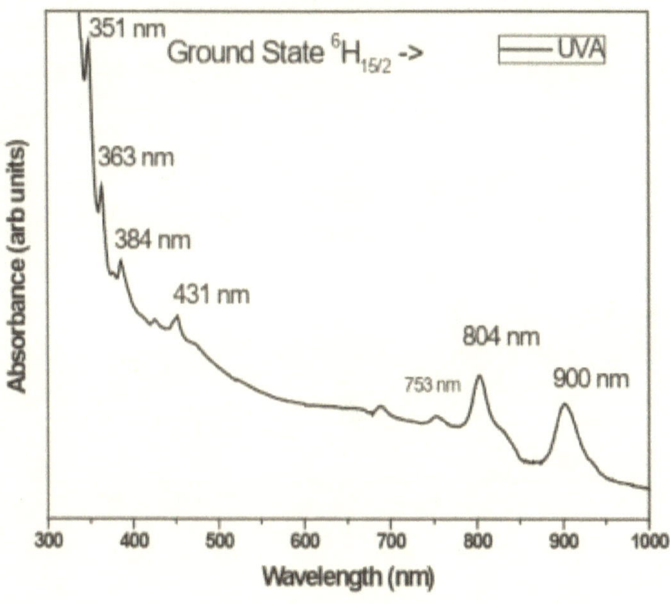

Fig 6.1: Optical absorption spectrum - UVA glass

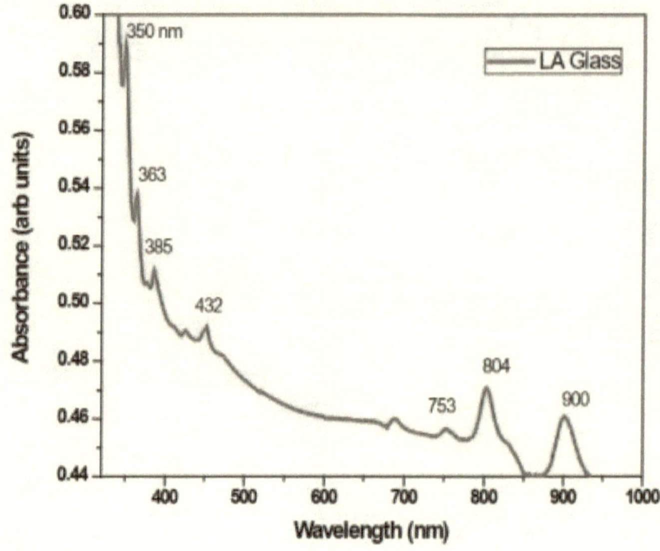

Fig 6.1a: Optical absorption spectrum- LA glass

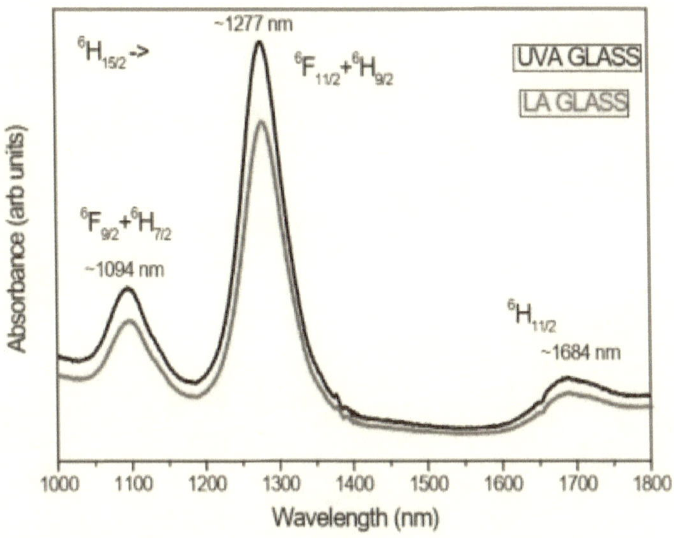

Fig 6.2: Absorption spectrum in NIR region for irradiated glasses

The J-O intensity parameters Ωk (k = 2, 4, 6) were evaluated from the observed absorption bands[12,13] and tabulated. It is well known that $\Omega 2$ parameter shows the covalency of metal-ligand bond and symmetry around rare earth ion. Further $\Omega 6$ parameter shows the rigidity of the host and also vibronic dependent [20,21].

6.3.2. Absorption studies of Pr^{3+} doped Irradiated glasses (UVB and LB glasses):

UV-Vis-NIR absorption spectra of irradiated metal phosphate glasses were present in Fig. 6.3 and Fig. 6.4. The bands observed were assigned for various transitions and were shown in figures. All the transitions were the characteristic bands of Pr^{3+} ions from its ground state $^3H4$ [22].

G. CHANDANA

10 | P a g e

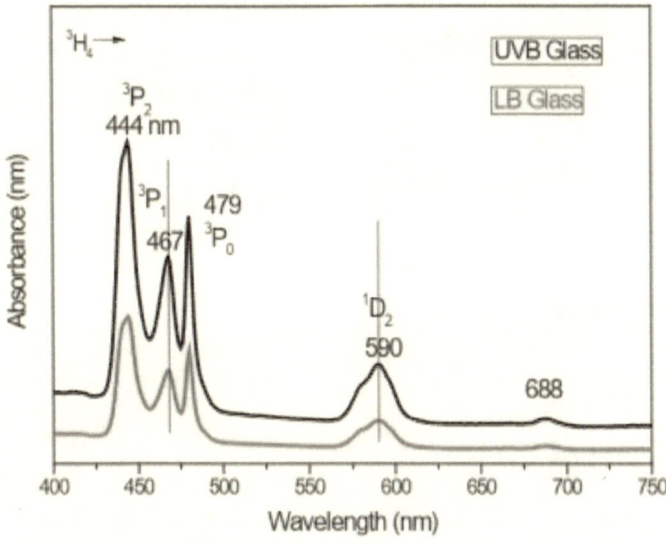

Fig 6.3: Optical absorption spectrum- Pr^{3+} doped irradiated glass

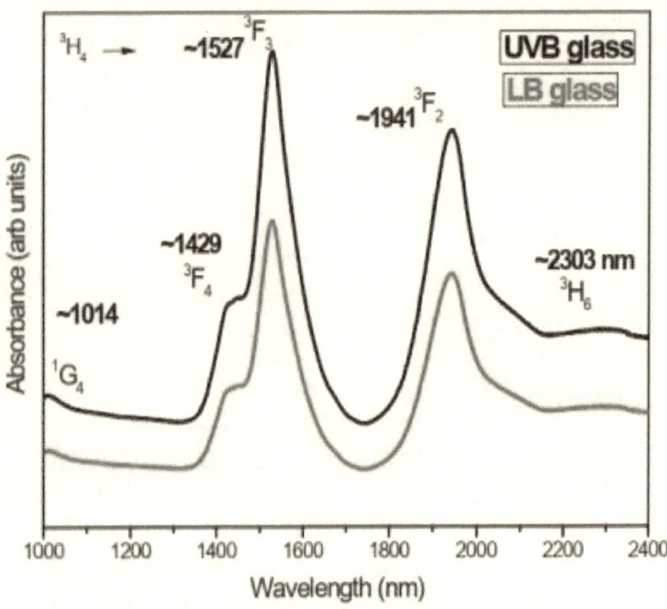

Fig 6.4: Absorption spectrum in NIR region for irradiated glasses

The J-O parameters were calculated for the irradiated glasses and compared with the pure glass. 4f2-intra-configurational electric dipole (ED) transitions to different excited states 3PJ=0,1,2 and $^1D2$ are the origin of the absorption bands. Unresolved Stark splitting and inhomogeneous broadening causes the broadening in the absorption spectra.

6.3.3. *Absorption studies of Sm^{3+} doped Irradiated glasses (UVC and LC glasses):*

Fig. 6.5 and Fig. 6.6 shows the optical absorption spectra in both UV-Visible region and NIR regions for both UV and Laser Irradiated glasses doped with Sm^{3+} ions. The characteristic Sm^{3+} absorption bands were observed and assigned the transitions from the $^6H_{5/2}$ ground state to different excited states. Various transitions from ground state to excited states - $^4F_{9/2}$, $^6P_{7/2}$, $^4F_{7/2}$, $^4I_{11/2}$, $^6F_{11/2}$ are at higher energy side and $6F_{9/2}$, $^6F_{7/2}$, $^6F_{5/2}$, $^6F_{3/2}$, $^6H_{15/2}$ and $^6F_{1/2}$ respectively [16] are at lower energy side were

assigned for the observed bands.

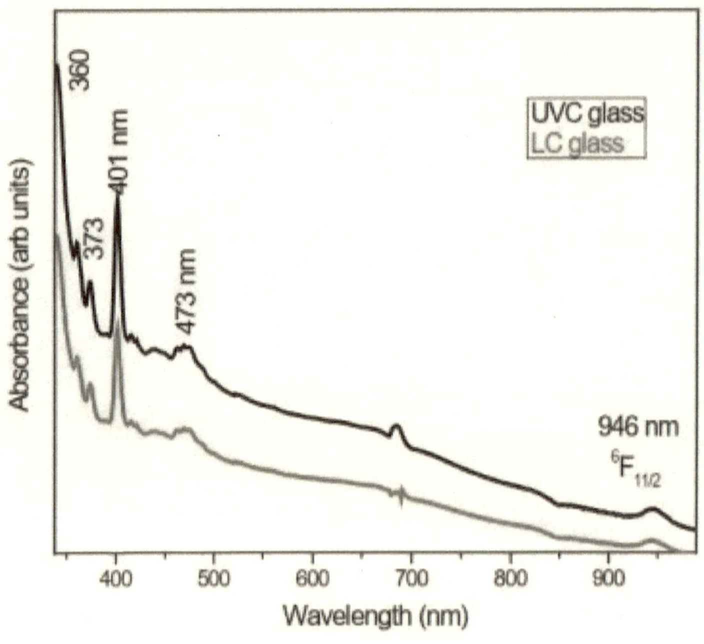

Fig 6.5: Optical absorption spectrum- Sm^{3+} doped irradiated glass

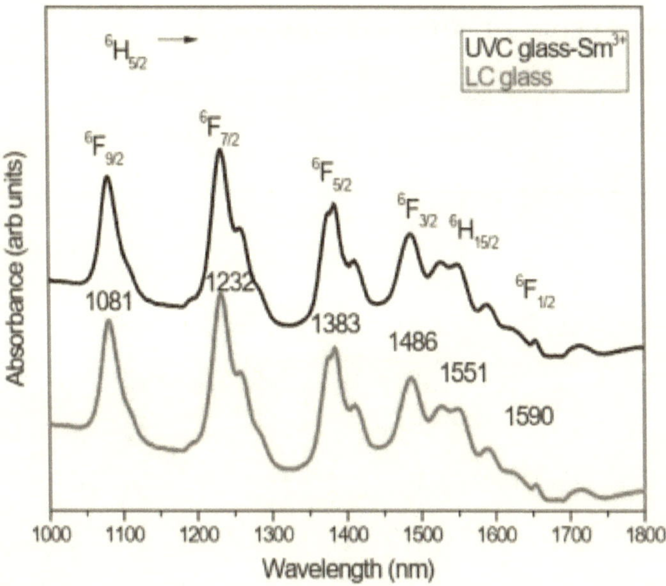

Fig 6.6: Absorption spectrum in NIR region for irradiated glasses

The J-O intensity parameters were evaluated from the absorption spectra and tabulated. These parameters follows, $\Omega2<\Omega6<\Omega4$ trend and is similar to other glasses and pure glass of current study. High covalency nature of the ion-ligand bond (Sm-O) is determined by $\Omega2$ parameter and also it explains the occupancy of asymmetry sites by Sm^{3+} ions in the host matrix [20s, 21]. Higher intensities in optical absorption spectra is a result of high mixing of the opposite parity electronic configurations.

Table 6.1 Evaluated J-O intensity parameters (cm^2)

Glass	Judd-Ofelt Intensity Parameters			Trend	Ref.
	$\Omega_2 \times 10^{-21}$	$\Omega_4 \times 10^{-21}$	$\Omega_6 \times 10^{-21}$		
A	0.736	0.223	0.0462	$\Omega_2 > \Omega_4 > \Omega_6$	Chap 3
UVA	0.729	0.225	0.0542	$\Omega_2 > \Omega_4 > \Omega_6$	
LA	0.653	0.342	0.0465	$\Omega_2 > \Omega_4 > \Omega_6$	
B	6.26	7.37	9.17	$\Omega_6 > \Omega_4 > \Omega_2$	Chap 4
UVB	5.43	6.99	10.41	$\Omega_6 > \Omega_4 > \Omega_2$	
LB	5.69	6.52	10.34	$\Omega_6 > \Omega_4 > \Omega_2$	
C	2.85	3.42	2.03	$\Omega_4 > \Omega_2 > \Omega_6$	Chap 5
UVC	3.12	3.22	2.89	$\Omega_4 > \Omega_2 > \Omega_6$	
LC	2.89	3.27	2.65	$\Omega_4 > \Omega_2 > \Omega_6$	

The evaluated J-O parameters shows a negligible variation in their values but it seems there is a variation by the irradiation. So, in estimating luminescence behavior, irradiation effects also accountable for change in luminescence efficiency.

6.3.4. Excitation and Emission Studies of irradiated Dy^{3+} doped metal phosphate glasses

Fig. 6.7. shows the excitation spectra of UV and Laser irradiated Dy^{3+} doped

metal phosphate glasses with 573 nm emission wavelength. At 348 nm, in excitation spectra, peak intensity is very higher than other peaks. So, it is opted as excitation wavelength to record the emission spectra of these irradiated glasses. The peaks observed were similar to the pure glass and with slight higher intensity.

Fig. 6.8. Shows the emission spectra upon 348nm excitation. It is with three characteristic emission peaks of Dy^{3+} ions in the present host. Intense emission bands obtained near to 483 nm, 574 nm and a feeble emission band near 663 nm are assigned to

the transitions $^4F_{9/2} \rightarrow {}^6H_{15/2}$, $^4F_{9/2} \rightarrow {}^6H_{13/2}$ and

$^4F_{9/2} \rightarrow {}^6H_{11/2}$ respectively and are similar to

the pure glass [23].

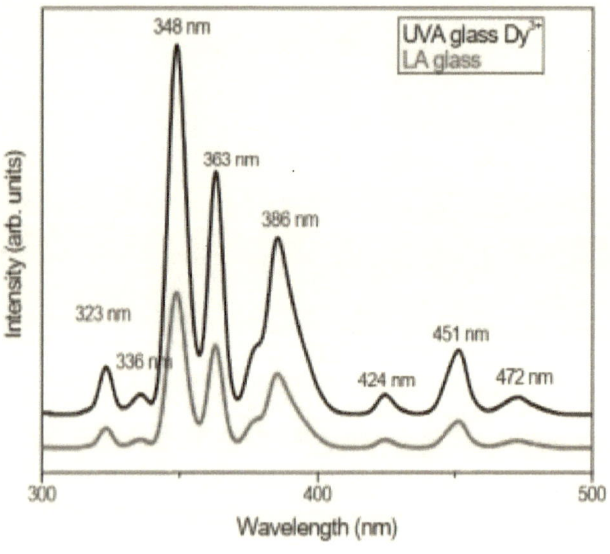

Fig 6.7: Excitation spectra – UV and Laser irradiated Dy^{3+} doped Metal Fluoro Phosphate Glasses (λ_{em} = 573 nm)

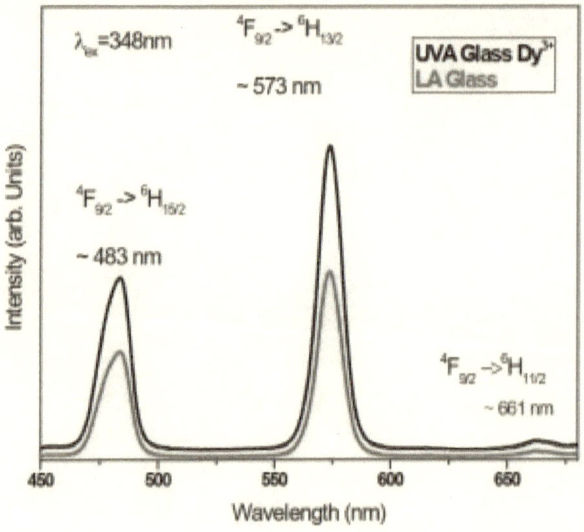

Fig 6.8: Emission spectra – UV and Laser irradiated Dy^{3+} doped Metal Fluoro Phosphate Glasses (λ_{ex} = 348 nm)

In the present irradiated glasses, the (Y/B) ratio

$(^{4}F_{9/2} \rightarrow {}^{6}H_{13/2})$ (yellow) /

$(^{4}F_{9/2} \rightarrow {}^{6}H_{15/2})$ (blue) is 1.54. It determines the white light emission. The emitting

photoluminescence of the present irradiated glasses are characterized by the CIE 1931chromaticity diagram [24,25].

The colour coordinates (x, y) for chromaticity diagram are evaluated as (0.34, 0.38) for UVC glass and (0.35, 0.39) for

LC glass. The co-ordinates shows white light region of CIE 1931 chromaticity diagram and is shown in Fig.6.13.

6.3.5. Excitation and Emission Studies of irradiated Pr^{3+} doped metal phosphate glasses

Irradiated Pr^{3+} doped metal phosphate glasses shows three intense excitation

bands by monitoring the emission at 607 nm. The bands were assigned to different transitions as at 441 nm ($^3H4 \rightarrow {}^3P_2$), 465 nm ($^3H4 \rightarrow {}^3P^1$, $^1I_6$) and 480 nm ($^3H4 \rightarrow {}^3P_0$)

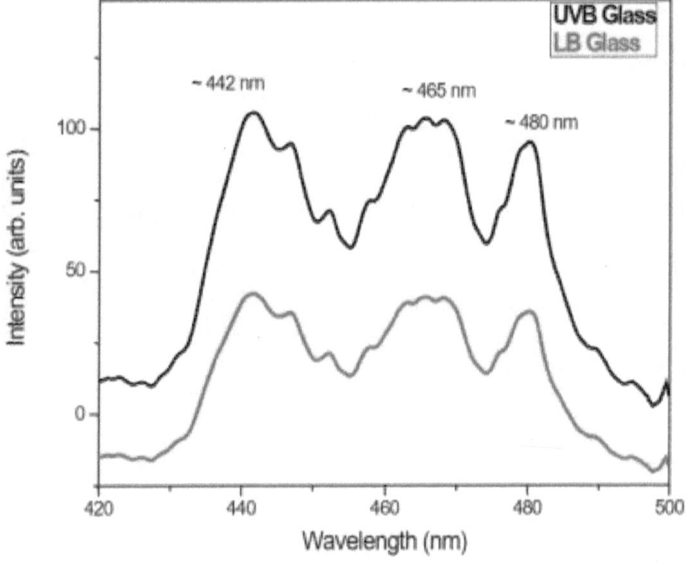

respectively [12]. The excitation spectra for the current irradiated glasses were shown in Fig. 6.9.

Fig 6.9: Excitation spectra – UV and Laser irradiated Pr^{3+} doped Metal Fluoro Phosphate Glasses (λ_{em} = 607 nm)

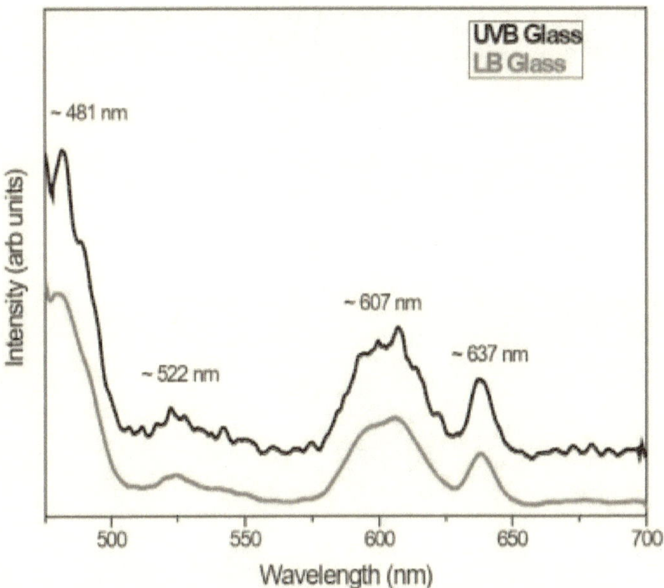

Fig 6.10: Emission spectra – UV and Laser irradiated Pr3+ doped Metal Fluoro Phosphate Glasses (λex = 441 nm)

The emission spectra were recorded for the current irradiated glasses by selecting the 441 nm as excitation wavelength as it has higher intensity in excitation spectra. The emission spectra consists of four bands and has higher emission intensity 607nm. The

bands are assigned to various transitions as 481 nm to

the transition $^3P_0 \rightarrow {}^3H_6 + {}^1D_2 \rightarrow {}^3H_4$.

The band observed at 522 nm is assigned to the transition $^3P_0 \rightarrow {}^3F_2$. The intense band observed at 607 nm to the transition $^3P_0 \rightarrow {}^3F_3$ and at 637 nm to the transition $^3P_0 \rightarrow {}^3F_4$ respectively [22]. The emission spectra are shown in Fig 6.10.

The emission for these glasses shows in red region. Therefore, these glasses are useful for red emitting material fabrications. The calculated CIE co-ordinates from the emission spectra fall in red region. The evaluated co-ordinates are (0.53, 0.26) for UVB glass and (0.54, 0.25) for LB glass. The CIE diagram and is also shown in Fig.6.13.

6.3.6. Excitation and Emission Studies of irradiated Sm^{3+} doped metal phosphate glasses

Excitation spectra were recorded with 597 nm as emission wavelength for the current Ultraviolet and Laser irradiated Sm^{3+} doped metal phosphate glasses and is shown in Fig.6.11. The excitation bands observed at different wavelengths and the corresponding transitions were shown in Fig. Here $^{6}H_{5/2}$ is the ground state. Further, the wavelength 399nm is choosen as excitation wavelength because of its higher population.

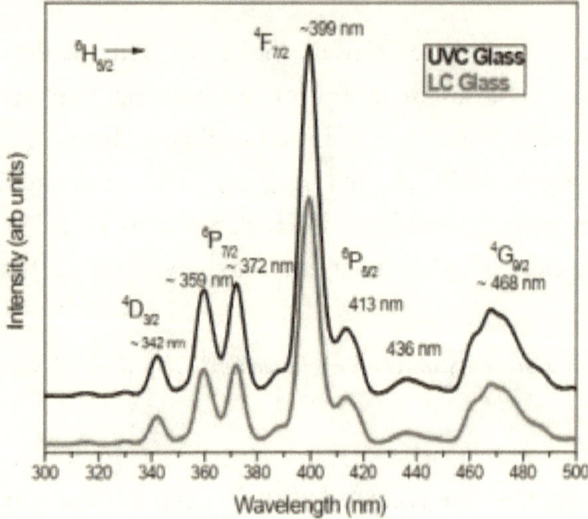

Fig 6.11: Excitation spectra – UV and Laser irradiated Sm^{3+} doped Metal Fluoro Phosphate Glasses (λ_{em} = 597 nm).

Here $^4G_{5/2}$ level is the metastable state and other higher states gives non radiative transitions and $^4G_{5/2}$ originates the emission spectrum for Sm^{3+} ions.

Sm^{3+} ion shows its characteristic emission features with emission bands in red region. The observed bands and the assigned transitions are shown in Fig. 6.12 and as

follows. Peak centre at 562 nm is assigned to $^4G_{5/2} \rightarrow {}^6H_{5/2}$ transition, band near to597 nm

to $^4G_{5/2} \rightarrow {}^6H_{7/2}$ transition. Lastly the band observed at 643 nm is assigned to the transition

$4G_{5/2} \rightarrow {}^6H_{9/2}$ [26–28]. All these transitions are in near to red region and the intense transition $^4G_{5/2} \rightarrow {}^6H_{7/2}$ shows a strong orange-red luminescence emission. Therefore, the

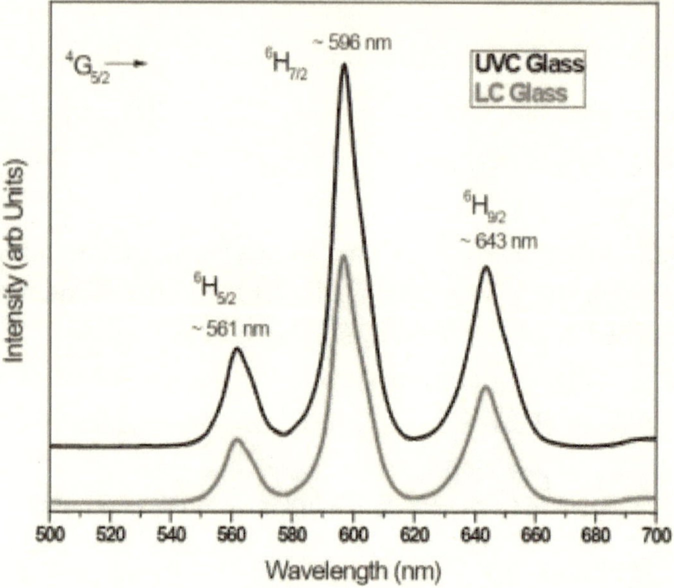

emitted radiative transitions which are observed for the current irradiated glasses matches with other reports on Sm^{3+} ions doped materials.

Fig 6.12: Emission spectra – UV and Laser irradiated Sm^{3+} doped Metal Fluoro Phosphate Glasses (λ_{ex} = 400 nm).

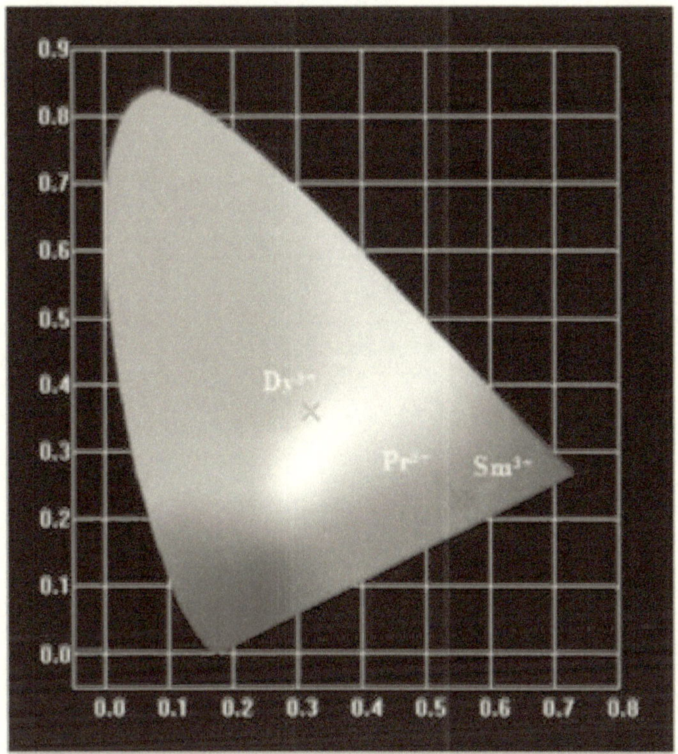

CIE chromaticity diagram has been used to estimate and evaluate the photoluminescence emission of current UV and Laser irradiated metal phosphate glasses doped with Sm^{3+} ions. The evaluated co-ordinates are (x, y) = (0.54, 0.25) for UV irradiated glass and (x, y)=(0.56, 0.24) for laser irradiated glass respectively. These coordinates clearly lies in orange red region and is shown in Fig. 6.13. Therefore, these materials can be useful for fabrication of red emitting devices.

Fig. 6.13: CIE chromaticity diagram for UV and Laser Irradiated Metal Fluoro Phosphate Glasses doped with Dy^{3+}, Pr^{3+} and Sm^{3+} ions.

6.4. CONCLUSIONS

The present Ultra Violet and Laser irradiated Metal Fluoro Phosphate glasses doped with various rare earth ions were shows good photoluminescence as by the characteristic natures of rare earth ions.

Amorphous nature of the current glasses were confirmed by the X-Ray diffraction. Though there is irradiation effects involved, it wouldn't changed the structural behavior of these metal fluoro phosphate glasses. Various bands were observed in Optical absorption spectra of Dy^{3+} ions doped irradiated glasses and the Judd-O-felt intensity parameters were evaluated for the bonding and symmetry of Dy^{3+} ions in the host matrix. Emission spectra shows the white light mission from the glasses and it is confirmed by the CIE chromaticity diagram.

Pr^{3+} ions doped metal fluoro phosphate glass was irradiated with UV and Laser sources and got very interesting results. J-O intensity parameters were evaluated and compared with pure glasses. The emission spectra shows the red emission with four characteristic emission lines.

Sm^{3+} ions doped metal fluoro phosphate glass is also studies with ultraviolet and laser irradiation. The absorption spectra shows the characteristic nature of Sm^{3+} ions in both UV and NIR regions. Excitation spectra and Emission spectra revels that these glasses emits the light radiation in orange red colour in the current glasses. Therefore, these glasses are useful in preparing red emitting materials.

So, the present work shows a new path to prepare and fabricate the materials which are useful for various kinds of optical and light applications.

References

[1] M. Yu, W. Zhang, G. Yan, S. Dai, Z. Qiu, L. Zhang, Warm white emission property of Ca2Sr (PO4)2: Dy^{3+} phosphors with red compensation by Eu^{3+} codoping, Ceram. Int. 44 (2018) 2563–2567.

[2] L. Yuliantini, R. Hidayat, M. Djamal, K. Boonin, P. Yasaka, E. Kaewnuam,Development of Sm^{3+} doped ZnO-Al2O3-BaO-B2O3 glasses for optical gain medium, (2017).

[3] V. Stelzhammer, S. Ozcan, G. Michael, H. Steeb, G.E. Hodes, C. Guest, H. Rahmoune, E.H.F. Wong, J. Russo, S. Bahn, Author's Accepted Manuscript, Diagnostics in Neuropsychiatry (2015).doi:10.1016/j.dineu.2015.08.001.

[4] K. Li, R. Van Deun,Accepted Manuscript 4+3+3+ (2018).doi:10.1016/j.jallcom.2018.03.292.

[5] P. Wang, M. Lu, F. Gao, H. Guo, Y. Xu, C. Hou, Z. Zhou, B. Peng, Luminescence in the fluoride-containing phosphate-based glasses: A possibleorigin of their high resistance to nanosecond pulse laser-induced damage, Sci. Rep. 5 (2015) 8593.

[6] J.E. Marion, M.J. Weber, Phosphate laser glasses, Eur. J. Solid State Inorg. Chem. 28 (1991) 271–287.

[7] A.N. Meza-Rocha, A. Speghini, J. Franchini, R. Lozada-Morales, U. Caldiño, Multicolor emission in lithium-aluminum-zinc phosphate glasses activated with

Dy^{3+}, Eu^{3+} and Dy^{3+}/Eu^{3+}, J. Mater. Sci. Mater. Electron. 28 (2017) 10564– 10572.

[8] S. Li, H. Liu, F. Wu, Z. Chang, Y. Yue, Effects of alkaline-earth metal oxides onstructure and properties of iron phosphate glasses, J. Non. Cryst. Solids. 434 (2016) 108–114. doi:10.1016/j.jnoncrysol.2015.12.004.

[9] S.N. Rasool, L.R. Moorthy, C.K. Jayasankar, Optical and luminescence properties of Dy^{3+} ions in phosphate based glasses, Solid State Sci. 22 (2013) 82–90.

[10] K. Jha, M. Jayasimhadri, Spectroscopic investigation on thermally table Dy^{3+} doped zinc phosphate glasses for white light emitting diodes, J. Alloys Compd.688 (2016) 833–840.

[11] U. Caldiño, A. Lira, A.N. Meza-Rocha, I. Camarillo, R. Lozada- Morales,Development of sodium-zinc phosphate glasses doped with Dy^{3+}, Eu^{3+}andDy^{3+}/Eu^{3+} for yellow laser medium, reddish-orange and white phosphorapplications, J. Lumin. 194 (2018) 231–239.

[12] Z. Mazurak, S. Bodył, R. Lisiecki, J. Gabryś-Pisarska, M. Czaja, Opticalproperties of Pr^{3+}, Sm^{3+} and Er^{3+} doped P2O5-CaO-SrO-BaO phosphateglass,Opt. Mater. (Amst). 32 (2010) 547–553.doi:10.1016/j.optmat.2009.11.011.

[13] G.V. Prakash, Absorption spectral studies of rare earth ions (Pr^{3+}, Nd^{3+}, Sm^{3+}, Dy^{3+}, Ho^{3+} and Er^{3+}) doped in NASICON type phosphate glass,Na4AlZnP3O12, Mater. Lett. 46 (2000) 15–20.

[14] Spectral investigations of Sm^{3+}-doped niobium phosphate glasses, Opt. Mater.(Amst). 66 (2017) 35–42. doi:10.1016/j.optmat.2017.01.027.6-24.

[15] G. Chandana, C. Nageswara Rao, P. Vasudeva Rao, M.J.S. Al-Musawi, K.Samatha,

G.G. Dhar, Luminescent properties of Sm^{3+} doped metal fluoro phosphate glasses, Optik (Stuttg). (2019) 163909.doi:10.1016/j.ijleo.2019.163909.

[16] D.D. Ramteke, A. Balakrishna, V. Kumar, H.C. Swart, Luminescence dynamicsand investigation of Judd-Ofelt intensity parameters of Sm^{3+} ion containingglasses, Opt. Mater. (Amst). 64 (2017) 171–178.doi:10.1016/ j.optmat.2016.12.009.

[17] J. Duan, S. Sun, Y. Zhang, J. Yu, N. Zou, A. Zou, Synthesis andphotoluminescence properties of KZnPO4: Dy^{3+}, Sm^{3+}, Optik (Stuttg). 201(2020) 163526. doi:https://doi.org/10.1016/j.ijleo.2019.163526.

[18] J. Pisarska, Optical properties of lead borate glasses containing Dy^{3+} ions, J.Phys. Condens. Matter. 21 (2009) 285101.

[19] K.N. Shinde, S.J. Dhoble, A. Kumar, Synthesis of novel Dy^{3+} activatedphosphate phosphors for NUV excited LED, J. Lumin. 131 (2011) 931–937.

[20] B.R. Judd, Optical absorption intensities of rare-earth ions, Phys. Rev.127(1962) 750.

[21] G.S. Ofelt, Intensities of crystal spectra of rare -earth ions, J. Chem. Phys. 37(1962) 511–520.

[22] K.A. Bashar, G. Lakshminarayana, S.O. Baki, A.-B. Mohammed, U. Caldiño,A.N. Meza-Rocha, V. Singh, I. V Kityk, M.A. Mahdi, Tunable white-lightemission from Pr^{3+}/Dy^{3+} co-doped B2O3-TeO2 PbO-ZnO Li2O-Na2O glasses,Opt. Mater. (Amst). 88 (2019) 558–569.

[23] W. Geng, G. Zhu, Y. Shi, Y. Wang, Luminescent characteristics of Dy^{3+} dopedcalcium zirconium phosphate CaZr4(PO4)6 (CZP) phosphor for warm- whiteLEDs, J. Lumin. 155 (2014) 205–209.

[24] R. Cao, K. Bai, X. Liu, W. Wang, T. Chen, S. Guo, Z. Luo, W. Li, Synthesis andtunable emission properties of Sm^{3+} and Mn^{2+} co-doped CaZn2P2O8phosphor, Opt. J. Light Electron Opt. 144 (2017) 591–596.

[25] S. Liu, S. Liu, J. Wang, P. Sun, Y. Zhong, J.H. Jeong, B. Deng, R. Yu,Preparationand investigation of Dy^{3+}-doped Ca9LiGd2/3(PO4)7 single-phasefull- color phosphor, Mater. Res. Bull. 108 (2018) 275–280.doi:10.1016/j.materresbull.2018.08.026.

[26] Z. Zhang, Y. Wu, X. Shen, Y. Ren, W. Zhang, D. Wang, Enhanced novel orangered emission in $Ca_3(PO_4)_2$: Sm^{3+} by charge compensation, Opt. LaserTechnol. 62 (2014) 63–68.

[27] R. Nagaraj, P. Suthanthirakumar, R. Vijayakumar, K. Marimuthu, Spectroscopicproperties of Sm^{3+} ions doped Alkaliborate glasses for photonics applications,Spectrochim. Acta - Part A Mol. Biomol. Spectrosc. 185 (2017) 139– 148.doi:10.1016/ j.saa.2017.05.048.

[28] V.R. Kumar, G. Giridhar, V. Sudarsan, N. Veeraiah, Influence of red lead on theintensity of green and orange emissions of Sm^{3+} and Ho^{3+} co-doped $ZnO–SrO– P2O5$ glass system, J. Alloys Compd. 695 (2017) 668–681.

******

Chapter 7 Summary and Conclusions

Now a day glasses are becoming very important material with different compositions in many preferred forms like lenses, screens, prisms and optical communication fibers which are in demand in regular life.

The rare earth (RE) doped glasses have great interest to study due their versatile applications in fabricating optical, storage and fiber amplifier devices. To know the information about the local environment of host matrix, Rare earth ions are well known probes with radiative transitions.

The host glass plays an important and interesting role in the development of RE doped optical devices. In view of the above applications extensive research has to be carried out for the search of new hosts doped with RE ions.

Therefore, in view of the current research on glasses, the present work has been carried out. In this, we investigated the influence of Metal Fluorides in Phosphate glasses doped with luminescence exhibiting ions such as Sm3+, Pr3+ and Dy3+ ions for lighting applications.

The composition of the glass matrix is

$$(60\text{-}x\text{-}y)\ P_2O_5 - 10CdF_2 - 15PbF_2 - 15NaF_2 - x\ Dy_2O_3 + y\ MgO$$

$$x=0.1,\ 0.3\ \text{and}\ 0.5;\ y = 0\ \text{and}\ 1$$

To prepare the glasses, melt quenching method have been choosen. Various characterization techniques like Optical Absorption, X-ray diffraction, Emission and

Excitation and Infrared spectra had been used to investigate the spectroscopic properties of the current Rare Earth doped Metal Fluoro Phosphate glasses.

X-Ray diffraction – Confirmed the amorphous nature of all the prepared glass samples.

Metal fluorophosphates glasses (Cd-Pb-Na) doped with Dy^{3+} ions were prepared successfully by using melt quenching method. Optical absorption spectra illustrates the characteristic features of Dy^{3+} ions in the present host. Judd-Ofelt theory was used to analyze the absorption spectra and discussed the various transitions. The transitions are well in agreement with theoretical and experimental values.

The Y/B ratios of Dy^{3+} doped Cd-Pb-Na fluoro phosphate glasses are in the white light range. The chromaticity colour coordinates are well placed. All the coordinates in white light region. Therefore, the prepared metal fluoro phosphate glasses doped with Dy3+ ions are useful for manufacturing of white light emission devices and as well as optical applications. The presence of MgO, the emission intensity is very high with no linearity condition in concentration. The influence of MgO is also prominent and the emission intensity is in trend as MP4 > P2 > P1 > P3. So MgO is playing the role of both intermediate and modifier in the present phosphate glass network.

Cadmium Lead Sodium fluoro Phosphate glasses doped with Sm^{3+} ions were prepared with composition was (60-x)

P_2O_5 – $10CdF_2$ – $15PbF_2$ – $15NaF_2$ – x Sm_2O_3 where x=0.1, 0.3 and 0.5 and investigated their optical properties and established crystal field effects on Sm^{3+} ion by addition of 1mol% MgO to the composition. The evaluated JO parameters followed the trend as $\Omega 2 < \Omega 6 < \Omega 4$ for all the prepared glasses.

12 | P a g e

The related branching ratio and emission cross section values were higher for MgSm5 than others. The emission transitions are in visible region from $^4G_{5/2}$ state. The

tranbsition $^4G_{5/2} \rightarrow {}^6H_{7/2}$ is dominant and is in red

region. Overall these glasses emits

orange-red colour upon excitation. By the addition of 1mol% MgO creates more defects as these atoms neither participate in network formation nor network modification. As a result, the environment around Sm^{3+} ion become more flexible for higher radiative emission in the present MgSm5 glass and is optimized. Hence these glasses were useful for preparation of Orange-Red light emitting devices.

Cadmium Lead Sodium fluoro Phosphate glasses doped with Sm^{3+} ions were prepared with composition was (60-x) P2O5 – 10CdF2 – 15PbF2 – 15NaF2 – x Pr6O11 where x = 0.1, 0.3 and 0.5 and investigated. In Optical absorption studies Hyperfine transition is not excluded from the results because of good fits in the J-O parameters. Concentration variation of oscillator strengths are clearly shown by these intensity parameters. In all the prepared glasses the J-O parameters have the values as $\Omega_2 > \Omega_6 > \Omega_4$. By the excitation of 442 nm, two emission peaks were observed in the red region by the transitions from $^3P_0 \rightarrow {}^3H_4$ and

$^1D_2 \rightarrow {}^3H_4$. From the calculated

lifetimes it is observed that the present host is the good for laser applications which will be operated at the wavelength of ~ 600nm. From the FTIR spectral studies, the spectrum reveals the fundamental frequencies of phosphate units From the above results it is concluded that the present host is suitable for sensitive red emitting lasers and fiber amplifiers with a marginal environmental changes.

Ultra Violet and Laser irradiated Metal Fluoro Phosphate glasses doped with various rare earth ions were shows good photoluminescence as by the characteristic natures of rare earth ions.

Amorphous nature of the current glasses was confirmed by the X-Ray diffraction. Though there is irradiation effects involved, it wouldn't changed the structural behavior of these metal fluoro phosphate glasses. Various bands were observed in Optical absorption spectra of Dy^{3+} ions doped irradiated glasses and the Judd-Ofelt intensity parameters were evaluated for the bonding and symmetry of Dy^{3+} ions in the host matrix. Emission spectra shows the white light mission from the glasses and it is confirmed by the CIE chromaticity diagram.

Pr^{3+} ions doped metal fluoro phosphate glass was irradiated with UV and Laser sources and got very interesting results. J-O intensity parameters were evaluated and compared with pure glasses. The emission spectra shows the red emission with four characteristic emission lines.

Sm^{3+} ions doped metal fluoro phosphate glass is also studies with ultraviolet and laser irradiation. The absorption spectra shows the characteristic nature of Sm^{3+} ions in both UV and NIR regions. Excitation spectra and Emission spectra revels that these glasses emits the light radiation in orange red colour in the current glasses. Therefore these glasses are useful in preparing red emitting materials. So, the present work shows a new path to prepare and fabricate the materials which are useful for various kinds of optical and light applications.

The spectroscopic investigation results of Dy^{3+}, Pr^{3+} and Sm^{3+} ions doped CdF_2

– PbF_2 – NaF_2 – P_2O_5 - Metal Fluoro Phosphate glasses shows the good photoluminescence emission properties by different excitation wavelengths corresponding to the ions.

It is concluding that the base CdF_2 – PbF_2 – NaF_2 – P_2O_5 - Metal Fluoro Phosphate glass host is suitable for all the rare earth ions for lighting, laser and optical window applications.

So, there is a lot of scope to work on this host composition with different intermediates and also with different Rare earth ions for not only lighting applications but also optical windows, fiber amplifiers and sensors etc.

Scope of the Future Work

The novel glass system Cd-Pb-Na fluoro Phosphate glasses were investigated in this work by doping them with different Rare Earth ions like Dy^{3+}, Pr^{3+} and Sm^{3+}. Using the same composition of the present systems, we are planning to prepare glass ceramics and we want to investigate their luminescent properties.

In general, Glass ceramics are a class of hybrid materials consisting of small crystals embedded in a glass matrix. If the dopant ions are inside the crystals, their luminescent properties are broadly those of ions in a crystal. If the crystals are much smaller than the wavelength of light, the material is optically homogeneous and thus transparent. The transparent glass ceramics, however, retain the material properties of a glass and can be processed and shaped with techniques used for glasses.

Glass ceramics are thus unique as they combine the spectroscopic properties of crystals with the manufacturability of glasses. It is evident from the literature that the luminescence efficiency possessed by the glass ceramics doped with rare earth ions are superior to their glassy counterparts doped with rare earth ions.

We anticipate some good results to come if these glasses doped with rare earth ions are systematically converted in to glassy ceramics and studied for their luminescence efficiency.

******

12 | P a g e

Chapter 7 Summary and Conclusions

Now a day glasses are becoming very important material with different compositions in many preferred forms like lenses, screens, prisms and optical communication fibers which are in demand in regular life.

The rare earth (RE) doped glasses have great interest to study due their versatile applications in fabricating optical, storage and fiber amplifier devices. To know the information about the local environment of host matrix, Rare earth ions are well known probes with radiative transitions.

The host glass plays an important and interesting role in the development of RE doped optical devices. In view of the above applications extensive research has to be carried out for the search of new hosts doped with RE ions.

Therefore, in view of the current research on glasses, the present work has been carried out. In this, we investigated the influence of Metal Fluorides in Phosphate glasses doped with luminescence exhibiting ions such as Sm3+, Pr3+ and Dy3+ ions for lighting applications.

The composition of the glass matrix is

$$(60\text{-x-y})\ P_2O_5 - 10CdF_2 - 15PbF_2 - 15NaF_2 - x\ Dy_2O_3 + y\ MgO$$

x=0.1, 0.3 and 0.5; y = 0 and 1

To prepare the glasses, melt quenching method have been choosen. Various characterization techniques like Optical Absorption, X-ray diffraction, Emission and

Excitation and Infrared spectra had been used to investigate the spectroscopic properties of the current Rare Earth doped Metal Fluoro Phosphate glasses.

X-Ray diffraction – Confirmed the amorphous nature of all the prepared glass samples.

Metal fluorophosphates glasses (Cd-Pb-Na) doped with Dy^{3+} ions were prepared successfully by using melt quenching method. Optical absorption spectra illustrates the characteristic features of Dy^{3+} ions in the present host. Judd-Ofelt theory was used to analyze the absorption spectra and discussed the various transitions. The transitions are well in agreement with theoretical and experimental values.

The Y/B ratios of Dy^{3+} doped Cd-Pb-Na fluoro phosphate glasses are in the white light range. The chromaticity colour coordinates are well placed. All the coordinates in white light region. Therefore, the prepared metal fluoro phosphate glasses doped with Dy3+ ions are useful for manufacturing of white light emission devices and as well as optical applications. The presence of MgO, the emission intensity is very high with no linearity condition in concentration. The influence of MgO is also prominent and the emission intensity is in trend as MP4 > P2 > P1 > P3. So MgO is playing the role of both intermediate and modifier in the present phosphate glass network.

Cadmium Lead Sodium fluoro Phosphate glasses doped with Sm^{3+} ions were prepared with composition was (60-x)

P_2O_5 – $10CdF_2$ – $15PbF_2$ – $15NaF_2$ – x Sm_2O_3 where x=0.1, 0.3 and 0.5 and investigated their optical properties and established crystal field effects on Sm^{3+} ion by addition of 1mol% MgO to the composition. The evaluated JO parameters followed the trend as $\Omega_2 < \Omega_6 < \Omega_4$ for all the prepared glasses.

The related branching ratio and emission cross section values were higher for MgSm5 than others. The emission transitions are in visible region from $^4G_{5/2}$ state. The

tranbsition $^4G_{5/2} \rightarrow {}^6H_{7/2}$ is dominant and is in red

region. Overall these glasses emits

orange-red colour upon excitation. By the addition of 1mol% MgO creates more defects as these atoms neither participate in network formation nor network modification. As a result, the environment around Sm^{3+} ion become more flexible for higher radiative emission in the present MgSm5 glass and is optimized. Hence these glasses were useful for preparation of Orange-Red light emitting devices.

Cadmium Lead Sodium fluoro Phosphate glasses doped with Sm^{3+} ions were prepared with composition was (60-x) P_2O_5 – $10CdF_2$ – $15PbF_2$ – $15NaF_2$ – x Pr_6O_{11} where x = 0.1, 0.3 and 0.5 and investigated. In Optical absorption studies Hyperfine transition is not excluded from the results because of good fits in the J-O parameters. Concentration variation of oscillator strengths are clearly shown by these intensity parameters. In all the prepared glasses the J-O parameters have the values as $\Omega_2 > \Omega_6 > \Omega_4$. By the excitation of 442 nm, two emission peaks were observed in the red region by the transitions from $^3P_0 \rightarrow {}^3H_4$ and

$^1D_2 \rightarrow {}^3H_4$. From the calculated

lifetimes it is observed that the present host is the good for laser applications which will be operated at the wavelength of ~ 600nm. From the FTIR spectral studies, the spectrum reveals the fundamental frequencies of phosphate units From the above results it is concluded that the present host is suitable for sensitive red emitting lasers and fiber amplifiers with a marginal environmental changes.

Ultra Violet and Laser irradiated Metal Fluoro Phosphate glasses doped with various rare earth ions were shows good photoluminescence as by the characteristic natures of rare earth ions.

Amorphous nature of the current glasses was confirmed by the X-Ray diffraction. Though there is irradiation effects involved, it wouldn't changed the structural behavior of these metal fluoro phosphate glasses. Various bands were observed in Optical absorption spectra of Dy^{3+} ions doped irradiated glasses and the Judd-Ofelt intensity parameters were evaluated for the bonding and symmetry of Dy^{3+} ions in the host matrix. Emission spectra shows the white light mission from the glasses and it is confirmed by the CIE chromaticity diagram.

Pr^{3+} ions doped metal fluoro phosphate glass was irradiated with UV and Laser sources and got very interesting results. J-O intensity parameters were evaluated and compared with pure glasses. The emission spectra shows the red emission with four characteristic emission lines.

Sm^{3+} ions doped metal fluoro phosphate glass is also studies with ultraviolet and laser irradiation. The absorption spectra shows the characteristic nature of Sm^{3+} ions in both UV and NIR regions. Excitation spectra and Emission spectra revels that these glasses emits the light radiation in orange red colour in the current glasses. Therefore these glasses are useful in preparing red emitting materials. So, the present work shows a new path to prepare and fabricate the materials which are useful for various kinds of optical and light applications.

The spectroscopic investigation results of Dy^{3+} , Pr^{3+} and Sm^{3+} ions doped CdF2

– PbF2 – NaF2 – P2O5 - Metal Fluoro Phosphate glasses shows the good photoluminescence emission properties by different excitation wavelengths corresponding to the ions.

It is concluding that the base CdF_2 – PbF_2 – NaF_2 – P_2O_5 - Metal Fluoro Phosphate glass host is suitable for all the rare earth ions for lighting, laser and optical window applications.

So, there is a lot of scope to work on this host composition with different intermediates and also with different Rare earth ions for not only lighting applications but also optical windows, fiber amplifiers and sensors etc.

Scope of the Future Work

The novel glass system Cd-Pb-Na fluoro Phosphate glasses were investigated in this work by doping them with different Rare Earth ions like Dy^{3+}, Pr^{3+} and Sm^{3+}. Using the same composition of the present systems, we are planning to prepare glass ceramics and we want to investigate their luminescent properties.

In general, Glass ceramics are a class of hybrid materials consisting of small crystals embedded in a glass matrix. If the dopant ions are inside the crystals, their luminescent properties are broadly those of ions in a crystal. If the crystals are much smaller than the wavelength of light, the material is optically homogeneous and thus transparent. The transparent glass ceramics, however, retain the material properties of a glass and can be processed and shaped with techniques used for glasses.

Glass ceramics are thus unique as they combine the spectroscopic properties of crystals with the manufacturability of glasses. It is evident from the literature that the luminescence efficiency possessed by the glass ceramics doped with rare earth ions are superior to their glassy counterparts doped with rare earth ions.

We anticipate some good results to come if these glasses doped with rare earth ions are systematically converted in to glassy ceramics and studied for their luminescence efficiency.

******

About the Publisher

www.ingramcontent.com/pod-product-compliance
Lightning Source LLC
Chambersburg PA
CBHW021151160726
47994CB00001B/152